paper
every day

LAURIE DEWBERRY

NORTH LIGHT BOOKS

Cincinnati, Ohio

www.artistsnetwork.com

About the Author

An avid papercrafter, Laurie Dewberry loves finding fun and inventive ways to incorporate paper arts into everyday life. In addition to her papercrafting work, Laurie has experience in communications, event planning and interior decorating. She is the author of *Creative Wedding Showers* and contributing author of *Retro Mania!*, both published by North Light. Along with her husband, Joel, Laurie is co-creator of The Paper Wardrobe line of scrapbook paper and the book *Paper Occasions*. She lives in Florida with her husband and three children.

10 09 08 07 06   5 4 3 2 1

Distributed in Canada by Fraser Direct
100 Armstrong Avenue
Georgetown, ON, Canada L7G 5S4
Tel: (905) 877-4411

Distributed in the U.K. and Europe by David & Charles
Brunel House, Newton Abbot, Devon, TQ12 4PU, England
Tel: (+44) 1626 323200, Fax: (+44) 1626 323319
E-mail: postmaster@davidandcharles.co.uk

Distributed in Australia by
Capricorn Link
P.O. Box 704, S. Windsor, NSW 2756
Australia
Tel: (02) 4577-3555

Library of Congress Cataloging-in-Publication Data

Dewberry, Laurie
  Paper every day / Laurie Dewberry.
    p. cm.
  Includes index.
  ISBN-13: 978-1-58180-840-7 (pbk. : alk. paper)
  ISBN-10: 1-58180-840-2 (pbk. : alk. paper)
  1. Paper work. I. Title.
  TT870.D45 2006
  745.54--dc22

2006009862

EDITORS: Jennifer Fellinger and Tonia Davenport
COVER DESIGNER: Marissa Bowers
DESIGNER: Stanard Design Partners
LAYOUT ARTIST: Stanard Design Partners
PRODUCTION COORDINATOR: Greg Nock
PHOTOGRAPHERS: Christine Polomsky, Michelle Brown and Tim Grondin
PHOTO STYLIST: Nora Martini
PAPER SAMPLES: Designed by Joel Dewberry

F+W PUBLICATIONS, INC.

Metric Conversion Chart

To convert	to	multiply by
Inches	Centimeters	2.54
Centimeters	Inches	0.4
Feet	Centimeters	30.5
Centimeters	Feet	0.03
Yards	Meters	0.9
Meters	Yards	1.1
Sq. Inches	Sq. Centimeters	6.45
Sq. Centimeters	Sq. Inches	0.16
Sq. Feet	Sq. Meters	0.09
Sq. Meters	Sq. Feet	10.8
Sq. Yards	Sq. Meters	0.8
Sq. Meters	Sq. Yards	1.2
Pounds	Kilograms	0.45
Kilograms	Pounds	2.2
Ounces	Grams	28.3
Grams	Ounces	0.035

DEDICATION

I dedicate this book to my three adorable children, Brendan, Brooke and Kirsten, who served as the inspiration and motivation behind making many of the projects in this book. It is for them that I love to infuse creativity into our everyday life, making it a little more interesting and memorable.

ACKNOWLEDGMENTS

A very special thanks to my photographer, Michelle Brown, for the many, many hours she spent working on the step-by-step photos for the projects in this book. Her flexibility allowed me to spend as little time away from my children as possible.

Also, many thanks to my editor, Jenny Fellinger, for her flexibility in allowing me to complete the book without having to travel, and for her planning and suggestions in organizing the book. And thank you to the stylists and designers who worked so hard to showcase the projects found on the following pages. I am grateful for the willingness of all these individuals to help me produce a successful creative work of which I will always be proud.

table of contents

❋ introduction {6}

Basic Tools & Materials 8

Techniques 10

❋ organizing {14}

"Mom's Diner" Dinner Planner 16

Nesting Storage Containers 20

Personalized Memo Clipboard 22

Art Supply Canisters 24

Greeting Card Organizer 26

Dial-A-Chore Chart 30

❋ celebrating {32}

Birthday Number Invitation 34

Purse Party Favor Box 36

"Tying the Knot" Bridal Shower Invitation 40

Birthday Countdown Frame 42

Flip-Flop Summer Party Invitation 46

Soccer Party Invitation 48

Butterfly Birthday Card 50

❋ giving {52}

Baby Journal Calendar 54

Pretty-in-Pink Gift Bag 58

Back-to-School Surprise Box 62

Lil' Baby Peek-A-Boo Card 66

New Neighbor Gift Bag 70

Thank-You Card 74

❋ remembering {76}

Family Reunion Memoir Album 78

Princess Keepsake Frame 82

Romantic Keepsake Box 86

Accordion-Fold Mini Album 88

CD/DVD Holder 92

Templates 110

Paper Embellishments 117

Paper Tear-Out Section 118

Resources 125

Index 127

❋ setting traditions {94}

Valentine's Candy Box 96

Fourth of July Party Invitation 98

Witch Hat Favor Cone 100

Thanksgiving Day Gratitude Book 102

Holiday Candle Holders 106

New Year's Countdown Place Setting 108

introduction

My idea behind *Paper Every Day* was to develop an array of paper-crafting projects that not only serve a practical purpose in our busy everyday lives, but also bring an added flourish of fun and creativity to every passing day—and, in doing so, make lasting memories. I have a friend who often says that, as a mother, she is "in the business of making memories." I like that outlook on life! But mothers are not the only ones who make and cherish memories. Married or single, parents or not, we *all* have a legacy to leave for our friends and families.

The projects in this book were created with a wide range of life events in mind, from the routine and most ordinary happenings to the rare and most special occasions.

All of these experiences create memories, which become even more vivid in our minds when they are tied to a tactile object, such as an invitation, a card, a decoration or some other item created especially for that moment in time.

For me, there is one thing that can make a handmade object really stand out: paper. I have a passion for paper. It is easy to work with, it comes in an endless selection of styles, and it is a relatively inexpensive indulgence. I have chosen to craft the projects on the following pages with various forms, styles and patterns of paper. In this adventure, I get to play with some of my favorites, and, in doing so, really showcase the versatility and possibilities of this wonderful

medium. Sometimes the projects were inspired after falling in love with a particular paper; other times the project idea was conceived first, then developed after searching for the perfect paper to communicate the intended emotion.

I hope this book inspires you to approach your everyday life in a new way and to look for ways to infuse a little more creativity into all that you do, be it planning a birthday celebration, organizing your office space or just making dinner.

Make every day beautiful!

basic tools & materials

To make the projects in this book, you will need to equip yourself with a few basic materials and tools. On the following pages, I've included a descriptive list of the essentials that I recommend keeping handy. Feel free to develop your own list of papercrafting "must-haves," as many of your most-loved supplies may be the ones you discover yourself.

PAPER

Paper is the most fundamental material for the projects. Get to know the kinds of paper currently on the market. The selection can be both overwhelming and inspiring!

Cardstock

Cardstock, sometimes referred to as coverstock, is heavier than text-weight paper but not as heavy as matboard or tagboard. It is available in many colors and patterns. The texture of cardstock ranges from smooth to heavily textured, and its finish ranges from matte to glossy. Cardstock works well as a base for all types of cards and invitations.

Text-weight paper

Text-weight paper is a medium-weight paper. It too is available in many colors, patterns, textures and finishes. To the delight of scrapbookers and papercrafters alike, an extraordinary array of decorative text-weight scrapbook paper is currently available. Many of these patterned scrapbook papers will be used for the projects in this book. Because text-weight paper is less substantial than cardstock, it works well when layered onto a piece of cardstock for invitations and other projects.

Translucent paper

Often called vellum, translucent paper is characterized by its see-through quality. It can be found in many colors and designs, and also is available in various weights.

Specialty printer paper

There is an ever-growing variety of specialty paper made for computer printers. Most of these papers are made for use in ink-jet printers. Two of my favorites are magnetic-backed and sticker-backed printer paper, which make it easier than ever to add custom-made decorative components to your crafting projects.

Heavy-weight materials

Heavy-weight paper products, such as matboard, tagboard and posterboard, are useful materials for boxes, covers and other projects that require a sturdy surface. Look for heavy-weight paper in packaging, and recycle it for your own projects. Tagboard, for example, is often included in packages of scrapbook paper to keep the papers from bending.

CUTTING TOOLS

A sharp blade can be the key to giving your project a sharp look. Invest in good-quality cutting tools for the best results.

Scissors

It is ideal to have two pairs of sharp scissors: a large pair for cutting down large sheets of paper, and a small pair for cutting out small pieces, images and embellishments. For quick and precise cutting of small pieces of paper, move the paper while keeping the scissors stationary as you cut.

Craft knife, metal ruler and self-healing cutting mat

A craft knife with a sharp, replaceable blade is essential. An all-purpose cutting tool, it allows you to make straight, sharp edges that cannot be made with scissors. Keep a supply of additional blades on hand to ensure the best possible cut. To protect your work surface, always work on a self-healing cutting mat when using a craft knife. When making straight cuts, run your knife along the edge of a metal ruler with a cork backing, which works well as a non-slip guide.

Basic tools and materials: cardstock, decorative text-weight (scrapbook) paper, translucent paper, specialty printer paper, heavy-weight materials, scissors, craft knife, metal ruler, self-healing cutting mat, paper punches, glue stick, spray adhesive, hot glue gun, sewing machine, embellishments

Paper punches

Hand-held punches work well for small pieces of paper, while a Japanese screw paper punch, complete with interchangeable hole sizes and a hammer, works well for punching holes in the center of larger pieces of paper (where a hand-held punch won't reach). A corner-rounder punch is another useful tool to keep handy, as it is an easy way to give projects a finished look.

ADHESIVES

There are many kinds of adhesives, each appropriate for different needs. Below are the most basic adhesives, which I rely on for almost all my projects.

Glue stick

This handy adhesive is suitable for gluing papers together. It is easy to use, dries clearly and is acid-free.

Spray adhesive

Stronger and more permanent than other paper glues, spray adhesive works well on papercrafts when a large, flat surface area needs to be covered with glue. It is an effective adhesive when you don't want the paper to shift during the gluing process.

Hot glue gun

Hot glue offers a stronger bond than glue sticks. It is the best choice when working with projects that are curved or heavier than normal.

SEWING MATERIALS

Some projects call for decorative stitching, which requires the use of a sewing machine. You need only a standard machine—nothing fancy! When adding decorative stitching to a paper-based project, just feed the paper through the machine as you would a piece of fabric. Experiment with different stitch styles and different colored threads for the look that works the best.

EMBELLISHMENTS

Embellishments are a fun way to dress up your projects. Ribbon, fibers, eyelets, stickers, tags—the list is endless when it comes to the possibilities for adding decorative details. Some embellishments, such as beads, stickers, tags and distressing ink, are simply decorative. Other embellishments, such as ribbons, brads and eyelets, are not only beautiful but can be functional, too. Instead of gluing layers of paper together, you can secure them with fancy eyelets or brads. And, to hold a party favor or card together, or to tie on a tag embellishment, you can use a length of pretty ribbon.

techniques

For the 30 projects in this book, you'll be using a wide assortment of techniques to produce great results. Most are common, simple techniques that you've probably used in other craft projects. On the following pages, I've explained a few of the basic techniques that I use more than once. If you are not familiar with them, they are not difficult to learn; just go through them step-by-step with the descriptions, and you'll be on your way!

SCORING AND FOLDING PAPER

Although scoring and folding is one of the easiest techniques in papercrafting, it is also one of the most important. Scoring and folding paper properly allows you to create a project with clean, crisp edges, giving it a more polished look.

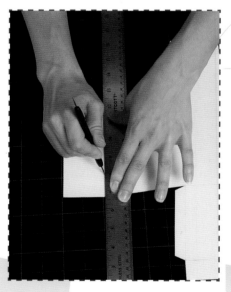

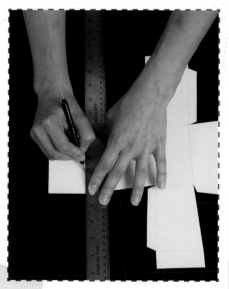

{1} Align scoring tool and ruler
When scoring a straight line along a marked measurement, be sure to place the tip of the bone folder or stylus on the mark, and the ruler directly next to the bone folder, along the marked line.

{2} Drag down scoring tool
Using the ruler as a guide, run the tip of the bone folder or stylus along the line, pulling the tool toward you as you apply even pressure.

{3} Crease along fold
Fold along the scored line, then crease the fold by flattening it with the body of the bone folder or stylus.

BEADING

If you thought beading was just for jewelry, think again! This popular papercrafting technique adds a touch of elegance and sparkle to any project. When combined on a paper surface, micro beads, seed beads and glitter make a marvelous beaded embellishment.

{1} Cover surface with beads

Place a piece of scrap paper on your work surface. Cover the sticky surface of an adhesive-lined paper with beads by sprinkling the beads over the surface and pressing on them to fill the entire space.

{2} Shake off excess beads

Shake the beaded paper over the scrap paper, allowing the loose beads to fall off. Carefully pick up the scrap paper and deposit the loose beads into a container, setting them aside for another project.

{3} Cover surface with fine glitter

Replace the scrap paper on your work surface. Sprinkle fine glitter over the beaded paper, allowing the glitter to fill in any gaps.

{4} Shake off excess glitter

Lift the beaded paper and shake off the loose glitter onto the scrap paper beneath.

SETTING CONCHOS

Conchos are small, metal embellishments with an open center. On the back, there are four sharp prongs, which are not as flexible as the prongs found on brads. If the paper is thin, poking the concho through the surface is not difficult. However, when the paper is a heavy-weight stock, it will help to use the simple process described below. The blunt end of a utility knife or other tool comes in handy for pressing the prongs flat on the back side of the project.

{1} Press concho into paper

Determine where you want to place the concho. Use the prongs of the concho to make identations on the paper, indicating the desired placement.

{2} Poke holes

Using a paper-piercing tool such as an awl or a needle, poke holes through the indented marks.

{3} Insert conchos

Insert the prongs of the concho through the holes. Turn the paper over, then press the prongs flat with the blunt end of the paper-piercing tool.

Every Day Tip

Work on your projects in an assembly-line fashion by completing one step at a time, like setting the conchos, for all of the finished pieces you need. You will stay better organized, and can "clean as you go," returning crafting items you are finished with back to their original storage place.

SETTING EYELETS

Eyelets are both practical and fun to use in almost any type of papercrafting project. With the wide variety of colors, shapes and sizes available, you can find eyelets to match any theme. Use these little gems as an anchor for layering paper, an embellishment in the center of a flower, a hole reinforcement through which to thread ribbon or other fibers, and more!

{1} Punch hole

Place your project paper on a self-healing cutting mat. Determine where you want to place the eyelet, then position the screw punch (corresponding to the size of the eyelet) accordingly. Hold the tool in a vertical position, then tap on the top of the punch with a hammer. Punch through all the layers to be held together at the same time.

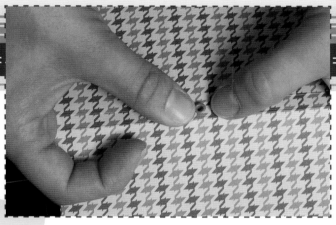

{2} Insert eyelet

Set the shaft of the eyelet through the hole, inserting it from the front to the back.

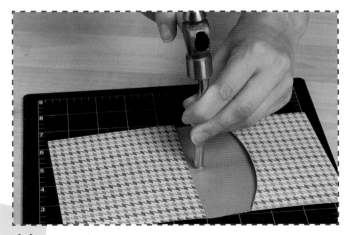

{3} Set eyelet

Turn over the piece of paper, with eyelet in place. Hold the eyelet setter tool upright, directly on top of the eyelet. Tap the setter with a hammer, allowing the shaft to spread to set the eyelet. Remove the setter, and gently tap the eyelet with the hammer to flatten it.

Every Day Tip

Eyelets are one of my favorite embellishing items, and I find I can never have too many on hand. When storing eyelets, brads and other little embellishments, keep a variety of colors in a container with small, divided sections to make it easy to select the ones you want.

organizing

With the busy pace of our lives, it is often difficult just to keep up with our everyday responsibilities, let alone find the time to do anything extra. Being organized is one way to better cope with the demands on our time. Why not take on the challenge of staying organized with some fun and simple papercrafts? The projects in this chapter have been designed to keep your everyday activities organized and to help you remember those important days, tasks and events that tend to sneak up on us.

"Mom's Diner" Dinner Planner

This magnetic meal organizer makes planning a week's worth of dinners a piece of cake! To streamline tasks, store your dinner planner and menu choice magnets on a magnetic board, along with a paper pad for keeping track of what food items you need to buy at the grocery.

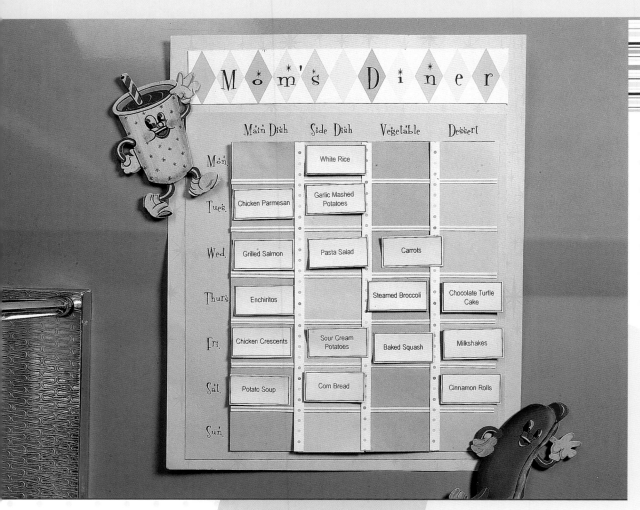

MATERIALS AND TOOLS

* decorative text-weight paper (all from the *Groovy Gal* collection, by SEI)

  rows-of-diamonds patterned paper (*Groovy Diamonds*)

  mini-polka-dot patterned paper (*Groovy Mini Dots*)

  multi-colored striped paper (*Groovy Pants*)

  pink starburst-patterned paper (*Twinkle Pink*)

  solid-colored text-weight paper

  cream paper

  light green paper

  light orange paper

  tan paper

  pink paper

* ink-jet magnet paper
* metal ruler
* scissors
* craft knife
* self-healing cutting mat
* spray adhesive
* glue stick
* computer (with a retro font, such as *Sparkly*, which can be downloaded from www.fontdiner.com)
* ink-jet printer

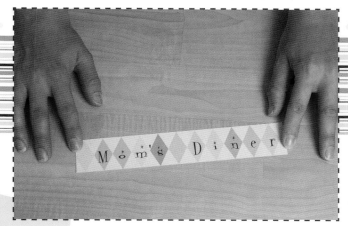

{1} Create heading

Cut a sheet of the diamond-patterned paper to 8½" x 11" (22cm x 28cm) and, using a computer, print the title "Mom's Diner" inside one row of diamonds. To do so, first measure in from the top and side edges of the paper to determine the correct paper margins. On your computer, create a document with the appropriate margins. Then, create text boxes the width and height of each diamond, approximately ¾" x 1½" (19mm x 38mm) for Groovy Diamonds. Using a retro font, spell out "Mom's Diner," placing one letter per text box. (For the Sparkly font, use a font size of 50 for the uppercase letters and 70 for the lowercase letters.) Print on the paper, then cut out the row of diamonds and set aside.

{2} Create weekly table

Cut a sheet of cream paper to 8½" x 11" (22cm x 28cm). Using a computer, create a table with the days of the week along the lefthand column and the headings "Main Dish," "Side Dish," "Vegetable" and "Dessert" along the top row, as shown. For my table, I made each table cell about 1¾" x 1¼" (4cm x 3cm). I also inserted the days of the week about ⅝" (16mm) from the left edge and 2⅝" (7cm) from the top, and the dish headings about 1½" (4cm) from the left edge and 1¾" (4cm) from the top. Print the table on the paper, then, using a craft knife and cutting mat, trim 1¾" (4cm) off the top so that the sheet measures 8½" x 9¼" (22cm x 24cm).

{3} Cut paper strips

With a craft knife and cutting mat, cut a 1¾" x 8½" (4cm x 22cm) strip from each of the following solid-colored papers: light green, light orange, tan and pink. Then, using the craft knife, make six tiny, evenly spaced notches on each colored strip to mark where the six thin strips dividing the days of the week will go.

{4} Cut magnet paper

With a craft knife and cutting mat, cut a piece of ink-jet magnet paper to 7" x 8½" (18cm x 22cm).

17

{5} Mount paper strips

Apply spray adhesive to one side of the four solid-colored paper strips from step 3. Mount these strips vertically, side by side, onto the black side of the magnet sheet.

{6} Cut first set of narrow paper strips

Using a craft knife and cutting mat, cut three 8½" x ¼" (22cm x 6mm) strips of polka-dot paper.

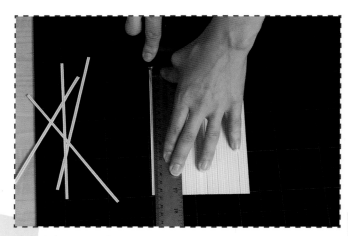

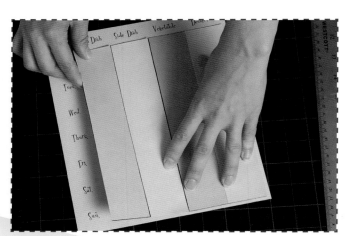

{7} Cut second set of narrow paper strips

Using a craft knife and cutting mat, trim six 7" x ⁵⁄₁₆" (18cm x 8mm) strips of striped paper, cutting along the direction of the lines.

{8} Mount magnet to paper

Apply spray adhesive to the back of the magnetic section prepared in step 5. Mount this section to the cream paper with the weekly table, lining up the left edge of the magnet with the left edge of the first column and the top edge of the magnet with the top edge of the first row.

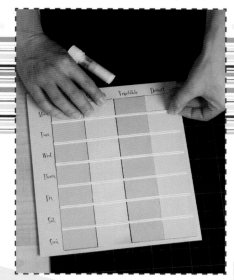

{9} Mount horizontal strips

Using a glue stick, mount the six striped paper strips horizontally across the four solid-colored strips at the marks you made in step three, covering the seams between the paper.

{10} Mount vertical strips

Using a glue stick, mount the three polka-dot paper strips vertically across the four solid-colored strips at regular intervals, covering the seams between the paper.

{11} Cut paper base

With a craft knife and cutting mat, cut a piece of pink starburst-patterned paper to 9½" x 12" (24cm x 30cm).

{12} Mount table and title to base paper

Position the weekly table and the title, centered, on the starburst-patterned base paper. Once you have the two pieces positioned correctly, mount them in place with spray adhesive.

{13} Print dish magnets

Using a computer and printer, design and print a selection of menu choices on ink-jet magnetic paper. To do this, I created ¾" x 1½" (19mm x 4cm) text boxes, entered a name of a commonly-made dish in each box, then color-coded each dish type to correspond with the color of the vertical row to which it belongs. Cut out each dish magnet and place it on the chart as desired.

Nesting Storage Containers

Add a designer's touch to your office space with these unique nesting containers. They take just minutes to assemble, which means you can make several sets with ease! Fill the containers with office items, such as sticky notes, paper clips and envelopes, and don't be surprised when your co-workers start admiring your newest desk accessories!

MATERIALS AND TOOLS

* 12" x 12" (30cm x 30cm) sheets of text-weight autumn-colored, double-sided (polka-dot/floral) paper (Harvest Small Daisies Chestnut, by Scenic Route Paper Company)
* brown satin ribbon
* green cording
* metal ruler
* stylus or bone folder
* scissors
* small hole punch

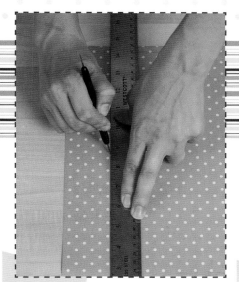

{1} Score paper

Place one sheet of autumn-colored, double-sided patterned paper on your work surface. Measure in 2" (5cm) from one edge of the paper, then score a line with a stylus or bone folder along the edge of a metal ruler. Repeat with the three remaining sides, running each score line all the way across the paper.

{2} Fold sides and pinch corner

Fold up the sides of the box along the scored lines. Pinch together one corner where the scored lines intersect, as shown.

{3} Punch hole through corner

While still pinching the paper together, punch a hole through the corner point.

{4} Secure corner with ribbon

Run a length of satin ribbon through the hole, then tie it in a bow to secure the corner. Pinch, punch and tie the three remaining corners in the same fashion.

{5} Create smaller container

Trim one sheet of autumn-colored, double-sided patterned paper to 9" x 9" (23cm x 23cm). Repeat steps 1–4 with this paper to create a smaller nesting container, this time using green cording to secure the corners. When finished, place the smaller container in the larger one, or fill each container as desired.

Personalized Memo Clipboard

Spruce up your personal work environment! Turn an otherwise mundane office item into a unique decorative element for your workspace, where you can hold papercrafting ideas, shopping lists, to-do lists and more.

MATERIALS AND TOOLS

* 8½" x 11" (22cm x 28cm) clipboard
* tracing paper
* decorative text-weight paper
  brown-on-brown swirl patterned paper (Dark Chocolate Swirl, by Chatterbox)
  pink-and-brown striped paper (Rosey Pedestal Stripe, by Chatterbox)
  blue-and-white ticking patterned paper (Table Ticking, by SEI)
* miniature frame with daisy pattern (Granny's Kitchen, by SEI)
* brown polka-dot ribbon (Granny's Kitchen Notions, by SEI)
* "dream" sticker (Granny's Kitchen, by SEI)
* daisy magnet (Target)
* pencil
* metal ruler
* scissors or craft knife
* self-healing cutting mat
* spray adhesive
* gluestick

{1} Cut tracing paper

Measure the base of the metal clip on your clipboard, noting its length and width. Mark the center top of a sheet of tracing paper with an inverted T that measures ¼" (6mm) longer and ¼" (6mm) wider than the clip base. Following along the lines, cut a T-shaped slit into the paper.

{2} Create pattern

Slide the sheet of tracing paper over the clipboard, fitting the flaps of the slit around the clip. With a pencil, trace around the base of the metal clip and the top and side edges of the clipboard. Cut along the traced lines to create the pattern for the next step.

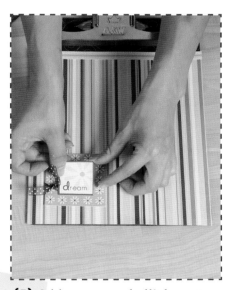

{3} Cover board with paper

Place a sheet of brown-on-brown swirl paper right side up on your work surface and place the pattern on top. Trace around the pattern, then trim the paper to size. Measure and trim a sheet of pink-and-brown striped paper to cover the surface of the board just below the clip. Adhere the brown paper to the clipboard with spray adhesive first, then adhere the striped paper on top.

{4} Add paper strip

Trim a strip of ticking-patterned paper to fit across the width of the clipboard. Adhere this strip just below the clip, covering the seam of the other two papers.

{5} Add corner embellishment

Tie a length of brown polka-dot ribbon around a daisy frame. With a gluestick, adhere this frame to the lower left corner of the clipboard. Add a "dream" sticker inside the window of the frame. If desired, add a decorative magnet to the metal clip.

Art Supply Canisters

These containers not only help keep you organized, they also inspire creativity with their playful look. Create a well-organized art space by using several of these paper-covered paint cans to hold crafty items, such as paintbrushes, pencils, markers and more.

MATERIALS AND TOOLS

* paint can
* decorative text-weight paper (all from from Ki Memories Collection V Playful)

    concentric-circle patterned paper (Playful Loops)

    large-dot patterned paper (Playful Palette)

* solid orange cardstock (Hazard, from Ki Memories Collection V Playful)
* ink-jet sticker paper
* 1½" x 1½" (4cm x 4cm) stitchable tin squares, with holes around the edges (Making Memories)

* green thread
* pencil
* metal ruler
* scissors
* craft knife
* self-healing cutting mat
* needle
* spray adhesive
* double-sided tape
* computer and ink-jet printer

{1} Cut decorative paper

Place the circle patterned paper face down on your work surface. Draw a 4⅝"-wide (12cm) strip on the diagonal of the paper, as shown. (The top edge of the strip should meet one of the paper's corners, while the bottom edge of the strip should meet the opposite corner.) Cut out the paper strip, using a craft knife and metal ruler on a cutting mat.

{2} Cover can with paper

Coat the back surface of the paper strip with spray adhesive. Wrap the paper around the exterior of the paint can, as shown.

{3} Add paper strip to can

Cut a 1" x 12" (3cm x 30cm) strip of the large-dot paper. Spray the back with adhesive, and wrap it around the can, placing it about one-third from the top.

{4} Make tag

Place a stitchable tin square on a sheet of orange cardstock, adhering it in place with double-sided tape. Poke holes through the paper with a needle, placing the holes evenly around the perimeter of the tin square and centering them between the existing holes of the square. Using the needle and a length of doubled green thread, zig-zag stitch the tin square to the cardstock. Trim the cardstock around the stitching, leaving about a ¼" (6mm) border of orange.

{5} Attach tag to can

Adhere the stitched square to the can with double-sided tape, placing it over the seam of the strip added in step 3. Using a computer, create a document with the name(s) of the items to be stored in the can, centering the word(s) within circular borders. Print the word(s) on a piece of ink-jet sticker paper and cut it out with scissors. Affix the sticker to the center of the stitched square. If desired, make coordinating cans of varying sizes to hold different supplies.

Greeting Card Organizer

With this personalized organizer, you will always be prepared with a greeting card to celebrate your friends' and family members' important events. The accordion-file system allows you to store birthday, anniversary and holiday cards by the month, making it a snap to remember every occasion.

MATERIALS AND TOOLS

* accordion-file folder, with orange book cloth along bottom spine (Target)
* decorative text-weight paper
  playful floral-patterned paper (Daydream Floral, by MOD Designs)
  striped paper (Daydream Stripes, by MOD Designs)
  large polka-dot patterned paper (Daydream Dots, by Autumn Leaves)
* solid-colored cardstock
  lime green cardstock
  light blue cardstock

* tagboard
* white printer paper
* orange thread
* metal month stickers (Inspirables)
* brad alphabet stickers (Making Memories)
* printed alphabet conchos (Colorbök My Type)
* pencil
* metal ruler
* scissors
* craft knife

* self-healing cutting mat
* spray adhesive
* double-sided tape
* glue stick
* sewing machine
* computer and printer

{1} Cut paper

Begin by removing the hardware and elastic cord from the accordion-file folder; put the folder aside. Using a craft knife and cutting mat, cut a 7" x 10" (18cm x 25cm) piece of the playful floral paper. Next, cut a 7" x 12" (18cm x 30cm) piece of the striped paper so that the stripes run horizontally along the 12" (30cm) width.

{2} Create paper strip with conchos

Cut a 1¼" x 4" (3cm x 10cm) strip of lime green cardstock. Mount five alphabet conchos along the center of the strip to spell "cards." (For instructions on setting conchos, see page 12.)

{3} Attach cardstock strip to floral paper

Using orange thread and a sewing machine set to a zigzag stitch, sew the lime green cardstock strip to the upper left edge of the floral paper, placing it about 1" (3cm) from the top corner.

{4} Create paper pocket

Place the striped paper horizontally on your work surface. In pencil, mark a vertical line 2½" (6cm) in from the right edge of the paper. Match the right edge of the floral paper along this line. Sew the papers together with a straight stitch just along the outer perimeter, again using orange thread and a sewing machine.

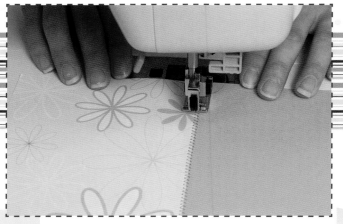

{5} Sew papers together

Cut a 5" x 7" (13cm x 18cm) piece of the floral paper and a
7⅝" x 7" (19cm x 18cm) piece of the lime green cardstock.
Line up the edges of the two papers, then overlap the floral
paper over the lime green cardstock by about ¼" (6mm).
Sew the papers together with a zigzag stitch, again using
orange thread and a sewing machine.

{6} Create month tabs

Using spray adhesive, mount an 8½" x 11" (22cm x 28cm) sheet
of polka-dot paper to a piece of tagboard. Flip the tagboard
over and mount one of the metal month stickers to the top half
of the board, leaving about ½" (12mm) of the board exposed
below the stickers. Repeat to make a tab for each month.

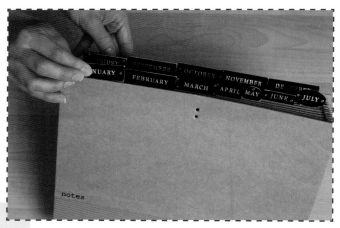

{7} Attach month tabs to folder

Run a length of double-sided tape along the exposed board on
each tab. Attach one month label to the back side of each pocket
of the accordion folder, starting with January in the front and
ending with December in the back.

{8} Create tabbed sheet

Cut a 10⅜" x 5¾" (26cm x 15cm) piece of light blue cardstock.
Place the cardstock horizontally on your work surface, then
create a tab along the left side by trimming about 1" x ½"
(3cm x 12mm) from each corner.

{9} Print and mount calendar

Use a computer and printer to create two 5½" x 9" (14cm x 23cm) calendars on white paper: one with the first six months of the year and the other with the last six months. With a glue stick, center and mount one calendar on each side of the light blue cardstock.

{10} Label tab

On the front side of the light blue cardstock (that is, the side with the first six-month calendar), add brad alphabet stickers to spell "calendar" on the tab.

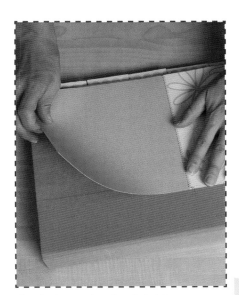

{11} Cover back of folder

Mount the sewn paper from step 5 to the back of the accordion-file folder with spray adhesive, placing the bottom edge flush with the top edge of the orange book cloth.

{12} Cover front of folder

Mount the sewn paper from step 4 to the front of the accordion-file folder with spray adhesive, placing the bottom edge flush with the top edge of the orange book cloth.

{13} Finish folder

Reattach the hardware and cord to the accordion-file folder. Slide the calendar into the pocket on the front of the folder.

Dial-A-Chore Chart

It's a snap to assign rotating household chores with this fun *and* practical Dial-A-Chore Chart. Divided into four sections, the colorful chart is designed for four family members. If you have more (or less) than four in your work crew, simply alter the design accordingly.

MATERIALS AND TOOLS

* scalloped circle template (page 110)
* decorative text-weight paper

    light blue polka-dot patterned paper (*Daydream Dots*, by Autumn Leaves)

    retro floral patterned paper (*Meadow Die Cut Flower*, by MOD Designs)
* cardstock

    solid orange cardstock

    solid lime green cardstock

    solid bright blue cardstock
* ink-jet sticker paper
* 1/8"-wide (3mm) preppy blue decorative tape (Heidi Swapp)
* rub-on letters (*Beetle Black Medium*, by Doodlebug Designs)
* bright blue brad
* pencil
* metal ruler
* compass
* craft knife
* scissors
* self-healing cutting mat
* glue stick
* computer and ink-jet printer
* photocopier

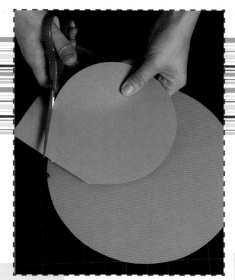

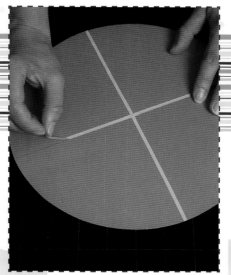

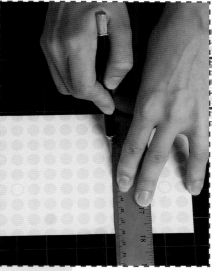

{1} Cut circles

Using a compass and pencil, draw a 9¾"-diameter (25cm) circle on orange cardstock and a 6⅛"-diameter (16cm) circle on lime green cardstock. Cut the two circles out.

{2} Add strips to circle

Using a pencil and ruler, draw a line across the diameter of the orange circle. Draw another line intersecting the first line at a 90° angle. Cover both with strips of blue decorative tape.

{3} Cut square

Cut a 4⅜" x 4⅜" (11cm x 11cm) square of light blue polka-dot paper.

{4} Assemble chart and add words

Trace the enlarged, scalloped circle template on a sheet of retro floral patterned paper, then cut out the shape with scissors. Layer the orange circle on top of the scalloped circle, followed by the lime green circle, followed by the light blue polka-dot square on top. Adjust the pieces so that all four layers are centered. Once the layers are in place, insert a brad through the center point. Use rub-on letters to label the square "Daily Jobs" and to label the lime green circle with family members' names, placing each name along one edge of the square, as shown.

{5} Add labels to chart

Using a computer and printer, lay out and print twelve chores, each within a 1⅜"-diameter (4cm) circle, on sticker paper. Cut out the 12 chore stickers. Adhere the stickers to the orange circle, placing three within each quadrant. Lay out and print four ½" x 1⅜" (13mm x 4cm) rectangles with the words "Done" on bright blue cardstock, and four ½" x 1⅜" (13mm x 4cm) rectangles with the words "Not Done" on lime green cardstock. Use a glue stick to adhere one cardstock rectangle to each flower petal, alternating between blue and green.

Note: *When finished, hang your chart on the fridge or another magnetic surface. Place a magnet on each person's section to move between the "Done" and "Not Done" labels.*

celebrating

A celebration is always something to look forward to, whether it's a birthday, wedding or another significant event. Whatever the occasion may be, we find joy in doing what we can to make it as memorable as possible. Festive, handcrafted projects are the perfect way to ensure happy and long-lasting memories. This section offers many ideas for such projects, starting with invitations, which set the stage for any celebration. Here you will find several "inviting" ideas to get you started with your party plans as well as ideas for helping others remember and celebrate significant events in their own lives.

Birthday Number Invitation

It's the "Big One"! This number invitation happily exclaims the significance of a child's first birthday. Not the first birthday for your little guest of honor? No problem! Just change the number to the appropriate age. For an easy party theme, incorporate that number into all the celebratory food and decorations.

bundles of sweetness,
Brightness and fun.
The beauty of springtime,
the warmth of the sun
And we're bubbling with excitement
Because they're both turning one!

Please celebrate Alyssa's and
Kirsten's first birthday with us.

Saturday, April 23rd
11:00 am,
Papa and Mima's pool

Materials and Tools

* white cardstock
* pink patterned vellum (*Pink Bubble Vellum*, by American Crafts)
* tagboard
* pink grosgrain ribbon
* scissors
* hole punch
* spray adhesive
* computer (with a playful font, such as *Sunshine*, which can be downloaded for a fee from www.twopeasinabucket.com) and printer

{1} Create and mount numbers

On a computer, create a large outline of the number representing the birthday being celebrated. Here, for a child's first birthday, I have created a "1" that measures 6½" (17cm) in length. Lay out the number as many times as possible on a single document, then print the document on white cardstock. Continue printing until you have the desired amount of numbers. Affix each sheet of cardstock to a piece of tagboard, using spray adhesive.

{2} Finish numbers

Lightly coat one side of a sheet of pink patterned vellum with spray adhesive. Adhere the vellum to one of the sheets of mounted cardstock, aligning the edges, then use your fingers to burnish the vellum in place. Repeat as necessary, covering each sheet of mounted cardstock with pink vellum. When finished, use scissors to cut out each paper-covered tagboard number.

{3} Design and print invitation text

On a computer, lay out the party invitation text within a 3¼"-diameter (8cm) circle, leaving some space above the text for two holes to be punched. Frame the text by outlining the circle in pink. For a decorative touch, add two smaller, overlapping circles—one light pink and the other dark pink—along the edge, as shown. Print on white cardstock as many times as necessary, then cut out each invitation text component, following along the perimeter of the design.

{4} Attach text to number

Position one invitation text component on top of a paper-covered tagboard number, centering the invitation as shown. Hold in place, then punch two holes, side by side, through the invitation text and the tagboard number. Thread a length of ribbon from the back, running one end of the ribbon through one hole and the other end through the other hole. Tie the two ends in a bow or knot, securing the two layers together. Repeat to finish the remaining invitations.

35

Purse Party Favor Box

If you're hosting a shower, tea party or girls' night-out, delight your guests with these stylish purse containers filled with candy or other goodies. Fun, whimsical and versatile, the charming favors are the perfect accessory to dress up any occasion.

MATERIALS AND TOOLS

* purse template (page 111)
* white posterboard
* decorative text-weight paper (all from the Sugar and Spice collection by EK Success)
* pink daisy-patterned paper (Sugar and Spice Double-Sided Flowers—Strawberry)
* striped paper (Sugar and Spice Double-Sided Shirt Stripe—Dots)
* ½" x 12" (13mm x 31cm) brown border sticker (Sugar and Spice)
* self-adhesive "Smile" epoxy tokens (Sugar and Spice)
* white Velcro
* pink thread
* pencil
* metal ruler
* stylus
* bone folder or other burnishing tool
* scissors
* craft knife
* self-healing cutting mat
* spray adhesive
* double-sided tape
* sewing machine
* photocopier

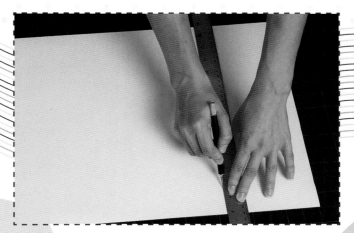

{1} Cut posterboard

With a craft knife and cutting mat, cut a piece of white poster-board to 14" x 17½" (36cm x 46cm).

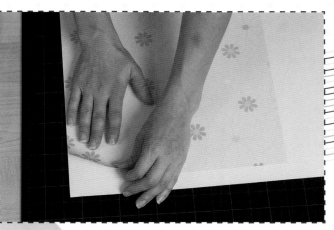

{2} Mount patterned paper onto poster board

Place the posterboard horizontally on your work surface so that one of the long sides is facing you. Measure in 1" (3cm) from the top and bottom edges of the board, then use a pencil to mark a horizontal line along both 1" (3cm) points. Using spray adhesive, mount a piece of pink daisy-patterned paper to the posterboard, lining up the top and bottom edges with the pencil lines and positioning the left edge flush with the left edge of the board.

{3} Create purse pattern

Trace the enlarged purse template onto the posterboard. Before doing so, position the template so that the flap will be on the plain white section of posterboard, not the paper-covered section, as shown. When finished, cut out the pattern.

{4} Add paper to pattern

Cut a 5½" x 5½" (14cm x 14cm) square of striped paper. Using a glue stick, mount this paper onto the flap of the purse pattern, lining one edge of the square flush with the daisy-patterned paper. With scissors or a craft knife, trim off any excess paper along the edges of the pattern.

{5} Score and fold purse

With a stylus, a bone folder and a metal ruler, score and fold the purse pattern, using the dotted lines on the original template as your guide. (For more instructions on scoring, see page 10.)

{6} Add purse closure

With a sewing machine, sew a small piece of white Velcro to the underside of the purse flap, at its center. Then, sew the corresponding fuzzy piece of Velcro (the same size) on the front of the purse, where the flap touches the purse.

{7} Create strap

Adhere a brown border sticker onto a scrap of white poster-board. Cut out the border, then cut it in half.

{8} Add handle to purse

Using a sewing machine and pink thread, sew the brown-border strap to the top flap of the purse, forming a handle.

{9} Assemble purse
Assemble the purse, folding the side flaps and securing them in place with double-sided tape.

{10} Embellish purse
Adhere a self-adhesive epoxy token to the front of the purse flap, positioning the token to cover the stitching.

The Art of Event-Planning

When planning an event, I start with a brainstorming session for papercrafting ideas. I love using paper for styling special events because it allows me to personalize the occasion without spending a fortune. The custom touch shows my guests I've put a lot of thought into the celebration.

Papercrafting a set of invitations or party favors for an event might sound like an overwhelming project, but by following these tips, you can enjoy a smooth creative process. The result: An event that all your guests will never forget.

✳ *Begin crafting your projects well in advance of the event so you can focus your attention on other party details in the few days leading up to the event.*

✳ *Decide what kind of mood you want to create for the event, then select your paper to match the mood.*

✳ *Figure out ahead of time how much paper you will need to create the necessary amount of projects for your event, and always plan on extra in case of mistakes or extra guests added at the last minute.*

✳ *Always practice your project on a piece of plain paper first to make sure you understand the instructions.*

✳ *Work on your projects in an assembly-line fashion by completing one step at a time for all the pieces.*

✳ *Instead of using a paper trimmer, try cutting your projects on a large self-healing mat with a craft knife and metal ruler. This this will give you more space to move around and more freedom to adjust quickly to the size you need.*

✳ *Save scraps of paper for future projects. Excess paper can be used for other projects, such as place cards.*

✳ *When working on a series of projects for an event, use the same colors, patterns, embellishments or motifs to tie the pieces together.*

✳ *Don't forget the details! Small details, such as the stitching on the Purse Party Favor Box, are what leave a lasting impression on your guests.*

✳ *Craft a special keepsake item for the guest-of-honor to take home. It will help her remember the event always!*

"Tying the Knot" Bridal Shower Invitation

Set the stage for a unforgettable bridal shower with this beautiful invitation. When planning the decorations and food for such a party, I always try to incorporate a motif or design element used on the invitation. In this case, it's easy—use the pink ribbon bows for a "tie-the-knot" theme.

MATERIALS AND TOOLS

* pink paisley/diamond vellum (The Paper Wardrobe Spring Sophisticates paper pad, by Plaid)
* solid pink double-sided paper (The Paper Wardrobe Spring Sophisticates paper pad, by Plaid)
* white cardstock
* pink satin ribbon
* metal ruler
* stylus
* bone folder or other burnishing tool
* scissors
* scallop-edged scissors
* craft knife
* self-healing cutting mat
* ⅛" (3mm) hole punch
* ¼" (6mm) hole punch
* spray adhesive
* glue stick
* computer and printer

{1} Prepare invitation base

Cut a piece of paisley-diamond vellum to 8" x 5" (20cm x 13cm). Use spray adhesive to mount the vellum on a sheet of white cardstock. Smooth out any air bubbles. Using scissors or a craft knife, trim the cardstock flush with the edges of the vellum.

{2} Create invitation insert

Using a computer, design the invitation interior within a 3¾" x 5½" (10cm x 14cm) text box, then print on a sheet of pink double-sided paper. (I printed on the dark pink side.) Trim the invitation insert to 3½" x 5½" (9cm x 14cm). Place the vellum-covered cardstock, pattern side down, in a horizontal position on your work surface. Mount the insert to the center of the cardstock with a glue stick, as shown.

{3} Make flaps

Place a ruler right along one edge of the invitation insert, then run a stylus along the ruler edge to score the white card-stock. Close the flap over the invitation, using a bone folder or other burnishing tool to crease the score line.

{4} Punch holes

Using a pair of scallop-edged scissors, trim the top and bottom of the invitation by ¼" (6mm). When finished, punch a hole in the center of each scallop with a ⅛" (3mm) hole punch. Close the flaps of the invitation. Punch two holes through the invitation with a ¼" (6mm) hole punch, centering one hole 1" (3cm) in from the left edge and the other 1" (3cm) in from the right edge.

{5} Finish with ribbon

Thread a piece of pink satin ribbon through the two holes from the back and tie a bow in the front, securing the flaps closed. Repeat steps 1–5 to make as many invitations as necessary.

Birthday Countdown Frame

Build excitement for an upcoming birthday with this Countdown Frame, fashioned after an Advent calendar. Place money, candy or other small items in the pockets, which can be opened one day at a time until the big day arrives. The large pocket can hold the "real" birthday gift—perhaps money or a gift certificate.

MATERIALS AND TOOLS

* small pocket template (page 112)
* large pocket template (page 112)
* square wood frame, with 12" x 12" (30cm x 30cm) opening
* decorative text-weight paper (all by Urban Lily)

    12" x 12" (30cm x 30cm) large polka-dot patterned paper (Frog Spots)

    12" x 12" (30cm x 30cm) striped paper (Freestyle Stitch)

    12" x 12" (30cm x 30cm) word-strip paper (Mountain Stripe)

* solid-colored cardstock

    light green cardstock

    turquoise blue cardstock

    brown cardstock

    light orange cardstock

* acrylic paint

    light blue

    white

* rub-on letters and numbers (Heidi, by Making Memories)
* personality word stickers (Design Originals)
* MetalGrams, white serif lowercase (American Crafts)
* orange brad
* ribbon (American Crafts)

    striped

    argyle

* orange thread
* pencil

* metal ruler
* stylus
* bone folder or other burnishing tool
* scissors
* craft knife
* self-healing cutting mat
* small hole punch
* stapler
* spray adhesive
* glue stick
* double-sided tape
* paintbrush
* sewing machine
* photocopier

{1} Prepare frame and insert

Before you begin, remove the cardboard insert from the frame and paint the entire frame white. After the paint has dried, paint the face of the frame blue, then distress it with white paint. Put the frame aside. Using spray adhesive, adhere a sheet of polka-dot paper to the cardboard insert.

{2} Make pockets

Trace the small pocket template (enlarged at 100%) onto sheets of blue and green cardstock; you will need five pockets of each color. Use a metal ruler and stylus to score the dotted lines on every pocket, then cut out each pocket. Using orange thread and a sewing machine, sew a straight-stitch border along the edges of each pocket square, as shown.

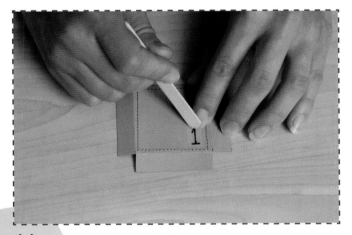

{3} Add numbers to pockets

Apply a rub-on number 1 in the lower right corner of a blue pocket square. Apply a rub-on number 2 in the lower right corner of a green pocket square. Continue applying numbers to the pockets in order, alternating between blue and green, until you reach 10.

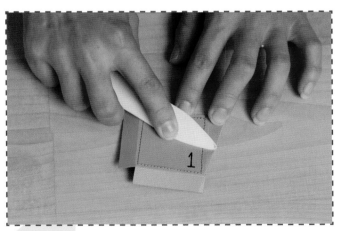

{4} Create side flaps

Using a ruler and stylus, score the diagonal dashed lines of one pocket. Fold back the resulting triangular section on each side, and use a bone folder or other burnishing tool to crease the dashed lines. Repeat with the remaining pockets.

{5} Add pockets

Place double-sided tape on the side flaps and bottom flap of each pocket. Adhere the pockets to the paper-covered cardboard insert, beginning 1" (3cm) from the top and ¾ (19mm) from either side. Space the pockets about ½" (12mm) apart and leave 1¼" (3cm) between each row.

{6} Create large pocket

Trace the large pocket template (enlarged at 133%) onto a piece of brown cardstock and cut it out.

{7} Embellish pocket with stitching

With a glue stick, adhere a piece of striped paper to the flap section of the large cardstock pocket. Using orange thread and a sewing machine, sew a straight-stitch border along the edges of the pocket. Fold the pocket along the center line (indicated by the dotted line on the template). Run a glue stick along the side and bottom edges of the back panel, then adhere the front and back panels to complete the pocket.

{8} Embellish pocket flap with stitching

Again using orange thread and a sewing machine, sew a straight-stitch border along the edges of the paper-covered flap.

{9} Add brad

Fold the paper-covered flap over the front of the pocket, then insert and secure an orange brad through the lower center point of the flap.

{10} Make note tags

Cut 10 small tags from orange cardstock, then punch a hole in the top center of the tags. Write a special message and adhere a personality word sticker to each tag. Thread a length of striped or argyle ribbon through each hole and staple the ribbon together.

{11} Add word strip to insert

Cut a word strip from a sheet of word-strip paper. Use a glue stick to mount the strip vertically across the cardboard insert, placing it below the last row of pockets and about ½" (12mm) from the bottom edge of the insert.

{12} Add pocket to insert

Use a glue stick to adhere the large pocket to the lower righthand corner of the insert, overlapping the word strip, as shown.

{13} Embellish pocket

Fit the finished cardboard insert inside the painted frame and secure the cardboard in place. Insert the note tags into the pockets, with the ribbon ends sticking out. Glue metal letters to the top and bottom rails of the frame to spell "Birthday Countdown."

Flip-Flop Summer Party Invitation

What is more fun than a bash to celebrate the beginning of summer? Get your party started "on the right foot" by sending this inviting flip-flop to your guests. They are sure to be a big hit—and they are super easy to make!

MATERIALS AND TOOLS

* flip-flop template (page 113)
* decorative text-weight paper

    flower-patterned paper (The Paper Wardrobe Summer Casual paper pad, by Plaid)

    V-striped paper
* cardstock

    solid white cardstock

    solid turquoise cardstock
* turquoise brad

* pencil
* scissors
* craft knife
* self-healing cutting mat
* glue stick
* computer and printer
* photocopier

{1} Make paper flip-flop

Glue a piece of white cardstock to the back of a sheet of flower-patterned paper. Lightly trace the flip-flop template (enlarged at 133%) onto the paper and cut it out. Cut a V-shaped strip from a sheet of V-striped paper. Using a turquoise brad, attach the center point of the V-strip to the top of the flip-flop cutout.

{2} Cut slits in flip-flop

Using a craft knife, cut two diagonal slits for the straps, using the dotted lines on the template as a guide.

{3} Secure straps

Slide the ends of the V-shaped strip through each slit to create the straps. Trim and glue the strap ends to the back surface.

{4} Print invitation text

Using a computer, design the invitation text, fitting it within a 2½" x 3" (6cm x 8cm) vertical rectangle. Print the text on white cardstock. Trim and glue it to a piece of turquoise cardstock. Trim the turquoise cardstock, leaving a ⅛" (3mm) border.

{5} Adhere text to flip-flop

Adhere the invitation text to the paper flip-flop, centering it at top, under the straps. Repeat steps 1–5 to make as many invitations as necessary.

Soccer Party Invitation

Upon receiving this sporty invitation, guests will be prepared to "have a ball" at your party! Don't be daunted by the complexity of the soccer ball design— a template makes it simple to reproduce.

MATERIALS AND TOOLS

* soccer ball template (page 113)
* cardstock
    * solid white cardstock
    * solid black cardstock
    * solid lime green cardstock
* walnut ink pad (Tim Holtz Distress Ink)
* pencil
* compass
* scissors
* craft knife
* self-healing cutting mat
* spray adhesive
* glue stick
* computer and printer
* photocopier
* optional:
    * lightbox
    * magnet paper

{1} Cut circles

Using a circle cutter or compass, cut two 4½"-diameter (11cm) circles out of black cardstock.

{2} Create soccer ball

Lightly trace the white parts of the soccer ball template (enlarged at 133%) onto a sheet of white cardstock. (A lightbox facilitates the process of tracing.) Cut out the pieces, then glue them onto one of the black circles, using the original template as a guide for where to place the pieces.

{3} Print invitation textd

Using a computer, design the invitation text, fitting it within a 3¾" x 2¼" (10cm x 6cm) vertical rectangle. Print the text on white cardstock and trim it to size. Run the surface of a walnut ink pad along the edges of the invitation to create a distressed look.

{4} Mount invitation

Use a glue stick to mount the invitation onto lime green cardstock. Trim the cardstock, leaving a ¼" (6mm) border of green.

{5} Slide invitation into ball

Using a craft knife, cut a 2¾" (7cm) horizontal slit in the paper soccer ball, about 1" (3cm) from the top. Run glue just along the edges of the the second black circle, then adhere it to the back of the soccer ball, lining up the edges. Slide the invitation into the slit. If desired, mount a piece of magnet paper onto the back of the invitation so the invitees can post it on their refrigerators as a reminder. Repeat steps 1–5 to make as many invitations as necessary.

Butterfly Birthday Card

There's nothing more thoughtful than presenting a good friend with a special handmade birthday card. This card couldn't be easier to make because the patterned paper and decorative cut-outs are right at your fingertips—in the back of the book. What a treat!

MATERIALS AND TOOLS

* butterfly template (page 113)
* decorative text-weight paper

    pink and brown floral patterned paper (Paper Wardrobe Boutique Pink Floral, page 119)

    pink diamond patterned paper (Paper Wardrobe Boutique Pink Diamond, page 121)

* cardstock

    solid white cardstock

    solid brown cardstock

* paper embellishment cutouts (page 117)

    pink border belt

    brown border belt

    "celebrate" word box

    pink decorative paper frame

* metal ruler
* bone folder or other burnishing tool
* scissors
* craft knife
* self-healing cutting mat

* small hole punch
* spray adhesive
* glue stick
* photocopier

{1} Create butterfly embellishment

Cut a 1¾" x 1¾" (4cm x 4cm) piece of brown cardstock. Center and trace the butterfly template (enlarged at 100%) onto the cardstock. Use a craft knife to cut out the openings for the body and wings, then use a small hole punch to punch the holes around the wings and along the antennae. Back the punched cardstock with a small piece of pink patterned paper (in the back of this book), securing with a glue stick. Trim along the edges of the cardstock.

{2} Prepare card

Cut a 4¼" x 11" (11cm x 28cm) strip of floral patterned paper (in the back of this book). Coat the back of the paper with spray adhesive, then adhere it to a piece of white cardstock. Trim the cardstock along the edges of the floral paper strip. Cut out an 11"-long (28cm) pink border belt (in the back of this book). With a glue stick, adhere the border belt to the floral side of the paper strip, parallel to the long end, about 1" (3cm) from the bottom edge, as shown.

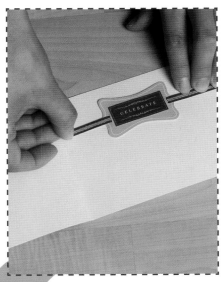

{3} Fold and embellish card

Fold the card in half, then crease the fold with a bone folder. Glue the butterfly embellishment on the front of the card, placing it on top of the belt border, as shown.

{4} Prepare word embellishment

Cut out a "celebrate" word box (page 117), then glue it to the center of a pink decorative paper frame (page 117). Use a craft knife to cut two small vertical slits on the frame, one on either side of the word box.

{5} Embellish card interior

Cut out a 5½"-long (14cm) brown border belt (page 117). Slide the belt through one slit on the pink frame, then run it through the other slit until the two ends are even. Glue the belt-and-frame embellishment to the right interior panel of the card.

giving

The most meaningful gifts are those we put a lot of thought into. An investment of time, thought and creative energy, handcrafted gifts always seem to fit this bill. They are one-of-a-kind and, because they come straight from the heart, handmade gifts truly express how much we care for the recipient. It is no surprise, then, that these gifts usually make the greatest impression. The projects in this section, which fall under the theme of "giving," will exercise your creative spirit and, in doing so, may just inspire you to give a little more of yourself.

Baby Journal Calendar

This journal's innovative design combines the handiness of a wall calendar with the charm of a memory album. Parents can track all of their baby's firsts on the calendar pages, and keep special cards, photographs and other mementos in the keepsake pages. Start with the month of the baby's birth and end with the same month—thirteen months in all—to track the entire first year of the child's development.

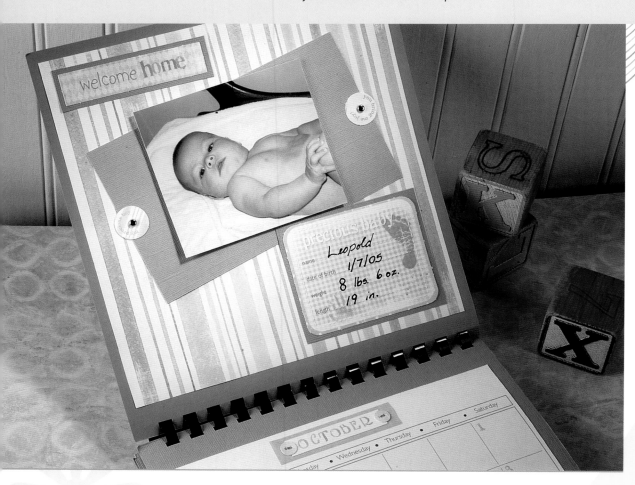

MATERIALS AND TOOLS

* light green text-weight polka-dot paper (Déjà Views Sharon Ann Collection Paper and Pieces Tablet)

* paper embellishments (*Baby Boy*, from Déjà Views Sharon Ann Collection Paper and Pieces Tablet)

    frames

    borders

    shapes

    tags

    clips

    die-cut letters

    die-cut buttons

* cardstock

    solid light blue cardstock

    solid white cardstock

* light blue ribbon

* orange thread

* number stamps (Hero Arts)

* alphabet stamps (Hero Arts)

* light blue ink pad

* metal ruler

* scissors

* craft knife

* self-healing cutting mat

* hole punch

* needle

* glue stick

* adhesive foam dots

* computer and printer, or marker

{1} Create calendar pages

Using a computer printer or a marker and ruler, create thirteen 7⅞" x 7⅞" (20cm x 20cm) calendar pages on white cardstock. (Leave space at the top of each page to insert the name of the month.) Go through each month of the upcoming year and, using light blue ink and number stamps, stamp the correct numeral date in the upper left corner of each day square.

{2} Make month labels

Using light blue ink and alphabet stamps, stamp the name of each month on white cardstock. Trim the cardstock around each month to a small rectangle shape, leaving about ¼" (6mm) space on the left and right sides. Glue these month cutouts onto scraps of light green paper and trim each piece, again leaving ¼" (6mm) space on either side.

{3} Sew buttons to month labels

With a needle and orange thread, sew paper die-cut buttons onto either side of each month label.

{4} Label each calendar page

Use a glue stick to adhere each month label to its corresponding calendar page, placing it in the top center.

{5} Mount calendar pages on cardstock

Cut fourteen 8½" x 9" (22cm x 23cm) sheets of light blue cardstock, then mount each calendar page to one sheet of the cardstock, leaving a ¾" (19mm) border at the top. You will have one extra page remaining.

{6} Create keepsake pages

Create a photo keepsake page for each month, using coordinating decorative paper, frames, borders and die-cut embellishments. Adhere each page onto the back of the cardstock calendar page that precedes that month. (See page 57 for sample keepsake page designs.) For the first month, mount the keepsake page on the extra piece of cardstock from step 5.

Note: When adhering paper frames, leave one side unglued so that the photo can be slid in at a later time.

{7} Begin calendar cover

For the cover page, cut out a 6" x 8" (15cm x 20cm) piece of white cardstock and a 8½" x 9" (22cm x 23cm) sheet of light green polka-dot patterned paper. Use a glue stick to mount the cardstock on the patterned paper, leaving a ½" (12mm) border of light green on the top, left and right sides and a 2" (5cm) border on the bottom.

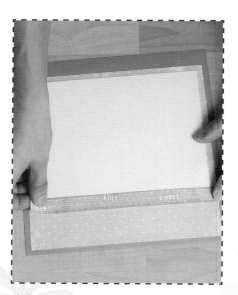

{8} Add paper strip to cover

Glue a blue border strip across the bottom edge of the white cardstock, covering the seam between the cardstock and the polka-dot paper.

{9} Add title to cover

Using adhesive foam dots, adhere die-cut letters to the white cardstock to spell "My First Year."

{10} Finish cover design

Glue letters on an oval tag to spell the baby's name. Punch two holes side by side at the top of the oval tag, then run a length of ribbon through the holes and tie a bow. Glue the tag to the cover in the lower right corner, as shown. Arrange the calendar pages in order, then have the calendar spiral-bound at a copy store.

Calendar Cover

One Month

Five Months

Eleven Months

57

Pretty-in-Pink Gift Bag

This beautiful bag makes an impressive presentation for any "girly" gift. When a creative fever strikes, construct several of these bags at one time, then use them throughout the year as your own signature gift bags.

MATERIALS AND TOOLS

* pink argyle-patterned text-weight paper (The Paper Wardrobe)
* white posterboard
* 3/8"-wide (9mm) white grosgrain ribbon
* pink die-cut tag (The Paper Wardrobe Spring Sophisticates paper pad, by Plaid)
* white thread
* pencil
* metal ruler
* stylus

* bone folder or other burnishing tool
* scissors
* craft knife
* self-healing cutting mat
* spray adhesive
* glue gun
* double-sided tape
* sewing machine

{1} Cut posterboard

Using a craft knife, metal ruler and self-healing cutting mat, cut five pieces of white posterboard: one 8" x 17" (20cm x 43cm) piece, two 3½" x 7¼" (9cm x 18cm) pieces and two ³⁄₈" x 14" (9mm x 36cm) pieces. Set the two ³⁄₈" x 14" (9mm x 36cm) strips aside for step 10.

{2} Mount patterned paper to posterboard

Cut an 8" x 12" (20cm x 30cm) piece of argyle-patterned paper. Use spray adhesive to mount this paper on the 8" x 17" (20cm x 43cm) piece of white posterboard, so that 5" (13cm) of the board remains uncovered, as shown.

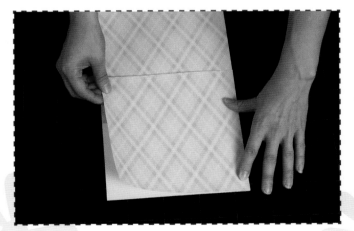

{3} Cover remaining posterboard

Cut a second sheet of argyle-patterned paper to 7" x 8" (18cm x 20cm) and mount it on the posterboard, covering the remaining 5" (13cm) left from step 2.

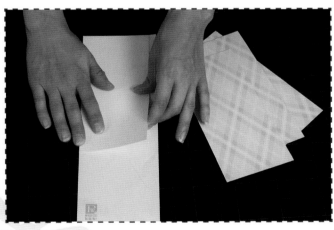

{4} Cover small posterboard pieces

Using spray adhesive, cover the two 3½" x 7¼" (9cm x 18cm) pieces of posterboard with scraps of the argyle-patterned paper. Trim patterned paper as needed.

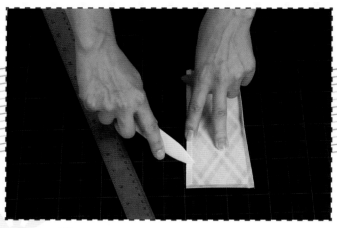

{5} Score and fold large board

Lay the large piece of paper-covered posterboard horizontally across your work surface. Using a stylus and metal ruler, score and crease one fold 7" (18cm) in from the left side and another fold 7" (18cm) in from the right side.

{6} Taper, score and crease smaller boards

Lay the smaller pieces of paper-covered posterboard vertically across your work surface. Measure in ¼" (6mm) from the left and right sides, and mark each point along the top edge with a pencil. Place a metal ruler on the posterboard, lining it up from the pencil mark on the upper left edge to the bottom left corner. Run a craft knife along the edge of the ruler, trimming the board so that it is tapered at the top. Repeat to taper the other side. Using a ruler, stylus and bone folder, score and crease a line ¼" (6mm) in from the bottom, left and right edges. Repeat the entire step with the other piece of paper-covered posterboard.

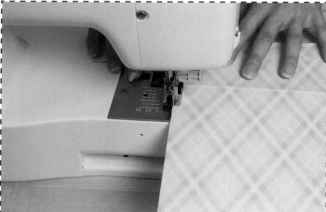

{7} Cut notches

Cut a square notch in the bottom left and right corners of the smaller paper-covered posterboards, where the folded lines intersect.

{8} Stitch border

Using white thread and a sewing machine, sew a straight-stitch border, with a ⅛" (3mm) allowance, around the large piece of paper-covered posterboard. When finished, sew a straight stitch ⅛" (3mm) from either side of the two creases.

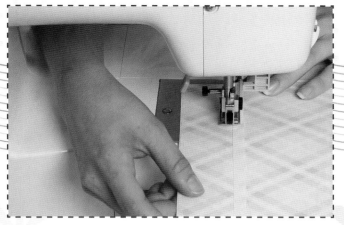

{9} Sew on ribbon

On the same piece of paper-covered posterboard, sew a length of white grosgrain ribbon about 2" (5cm) from the edge of each short end.

{10} Attach handles

Use the ³⁄₈" x 14" (9mm x 36cm) strips of posterboard to create one handle above each length of grosgrain ribbon. To do so, hold one of the strips vertically, perpendicular to the ribbon. Place the strip 2" (5cm) in from the left edge of the paper-covered posterboard, overlapping the board by about ⁷⁄₈" (22mm); sew in place with white thread. Bring the strip around to form a curved handle, and sew it in place about 2" (5cm) in from the right edge, again overlapping the board by about ⁷⁄₈" (22mm). Repeat on the other end to complete the pair of handles.

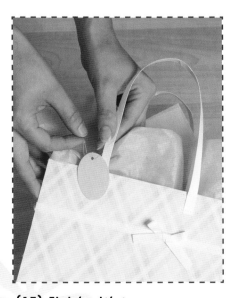

{11} Form purse

Fold up both handled sides of the paper-covered posterboard to form a purse. Add a line of hot glue to the scored sections of the smaller posterboard pieces, then adhere them to the corresponding side and bottom edges of the purse, forming closed sides.

{12} Attach bow

Cut a length of white grosgrain ribbon and fashion a small bow. Adhere this bow to the front of the purse with double-sided tape, placing it on top of the ribbon already attached to the purse, as shown.

{13} Finish with tag

Attach a pink die-cut tag to the top strap of the purse with a piece of white thread.

Back-to-School Surprise Box

When the summer days draw to a close, surprise a student or teacher you know with this clever handmade box. Send them back to the classroom in style, equipped with a stash of cool school supplies and other goodies!

MATERIALS AND TOOLS

* tag template (page 112)
* decorative text-weight paper patterned with elementary school-style writing lines (Writing Paper, by Karen Foster)
* solid brick-red cardstock
* tagboard
* printed alphabet conchos (Colorbök)
* printed twill ribbon
* "school" tag (Making Memories Signage Petite)
* walnut ink pad (Tim Holtz Distress Ink)
* black chalkboard spray paint

* white chalk
* pencil
* metal ruler
* bone folder or other burnishing tool
* scissors
* craft knife
* self-healing cutting mat
* hole punch
* spray adhesive
* hot glue gun
* double-sided tape

{1} Mount cardstock to writing paper

Mount a piece of brick-red cardstock to the back of the writing paper with spray adhesive, aligning the edges.

{2} Mount patterned paper to posterboard

On the brick-red side of the paper, draw four intersecting lines—one line 4" (10cm) in from each edge, as shown. These lines will create a grid.

{3} Cut paper

Using a craft knife, metal ruler and self-healing cutting mat, cut along the two vertical lines in the bottom section; stop cutting where the lines intersect with the lower horizontal line. In the same manner, cut along the pair of vertical lines in the top section, stopping where the lines intersect with the upper horizontal line. There should now be three flaps on top and three flaps on bottom, separated by a center strip.

{4} Cover small posterboard pieces

Fold each flap over, following the fold along the pencil line. Crease each fold with a bone folder. There should now be six folded flaps in all.

{5} Fold and secure box

Holding the center flaps straight up, fold in each set of flaps to create a box. One side of the box will serve as the front; when folding in the flaps, make sure the writing lines on this front flap run horizontally. Secure the box by adhering the layers of paper with double-sided tape; on the front flap, adhere only the bottom and left edges, as shown, so you will be able to fold the top down later in step 7.

{6} Ink edges

Run the surface of an ink pad along the edges of the paper box to give it a slightly distressed appearance.

{7} Fold corner of front flap

Fold down the top left corner of the front flap and push an alphabet concho through the brick-red side of the paper. Secure the concho by flattening the metal prongs on the other side of the paper. (For more instruction on setting conchos, see page 12.)

{8} Create pocket

Once the concho is in place, use hot glue to secure the corner of the folded flap to the box. This will create a pocket on the front side.

{9} Prepare tag

Paint a piece of tagboard with black chalkboard spray paint. Allow the paint to dry, then use a pencil to trace the tag template (enlarged at 100%) onto the board.

{10} Cut tag

Cut out the traced tag, following along the pencil lines. With a hole punch, punch a hole in the top of the tag, as shown.

{11} Distress tag

Run a piece of white chalk along the edges of the tag, as shown, then rub the chalk in with your fingers to give the tag a distressed look. When finished, write a back-to-school message, such as "Good Luck!", in chalk on the tag.

{12} Finish box

Run a length of printed twill ribbon through the hole of the tag and tie in a knot. Trim the ends of the ribbon as desired. Slide the tag in the front folded pocket of the paper box. Embellish the box with a small "school" tag along the bottom of the front side. Fill the box with school supplies, such as glue, pencils and a small composition book.

Lil' Baby Peek-A-Boo Card

This adorable card is sure to delight the mother-to-be before her little one arrives. Is the stork delivering a baby girl? Simply change the light blue tag to pink! Or, if it's going to be a surprise, keep the colors a neutral pastel.

MATERIALS AND TOOLS

* scallop template (page 114)
* pastel striped text-weight paper (The Paper Wardrobe Spring Sophisticates paper pad, by Plaid)
* cardstock
    solid white cardstock
    green linen cardstock (The Paper Wardrobe Spring Sophisticates paper pad, by Plaid)
* light blue die-cut circle tag (The Paper Wardrobe Spring Sophisticates paper pad, by Plaid)
* blue thread

* pastel green safety pin (Making Memories)
* colored chalk
* pencil
* metal ruler
* bone folder or other burnishing tool
* scissors
* craft knife
* self-healing cutting mat
* glue stick
* adhesive foam dots
* cotton swab

* computer, with:
    playful font, such as David Walker Oh Baby font, which can be downloaded for a fee from www.twopeasinabucket.com
    graphic font, such as Think Small font, which can be downloaded for a fee from www.twopeasinabucket.com
* printer
* sewing machine
* photocopier

{1} Print card interior text

Using a computer, create a document with a vertical 5"
x 9" (13cm x 23cm) text box. Create the interior text of
the card—"Just a sneak peak before your little one arrives.
Congratulations!"—in the bottom half of the text box, using
Think Small font or another font of your choice. Print on a
sheet of white cardstock, and trim along the perimeter of the
text box.

{2} Scallop edges

With a pencil, trace the scallop template (enlarged at 133%)
along the top and bottom edges of the card. Cut along the lines
to create scalloped edges.

{3} Print card exterior text

Cut a piece of green linen cardstock to 8½" x 11" (22cm x
28cm). Using a computer, create a vertical 8" x 5" (20cm x
13cm) text box. Insert the word "Peekaboo" in Think Small font
or another font of your choice, about 1¾" (4cm) above the bottom edge of the box. Print it on the green linen cardstock and
trim along the perimeter of the text box.

{4} Scallop edges

Trace the scallop pattern (enlarged at 133%) along the top and
bottom edges of the cardstock. Cut out along the lines to create scalloped edges. With a craft knife and metal ruler, slice a 2"
(5cm) horizontal slit just above the word "Peekaboo."

{5} Stitch border

Using blue thread and a sewing machine, sew a straight-stitch border along the edges of the green linen cardstock.

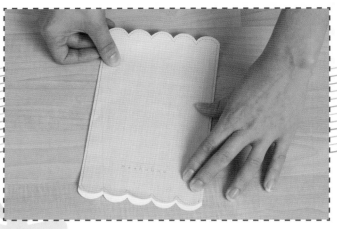

{6} Adhere two papers

Place the white cardstock card on your work surface, text side down. Run a glue stick over the back of the green linen card-stock, avoiding any area around or below the slit (later, this area will need to be clear for a sliding tag). Adhere the green linen cardstock to the white cardstock, aligning the side and top edges so that there is about ½" (12mm) of white showing along the bottom scalloped edge.

{7} Fold card

Fold the card in half and crease the fold with a bone folder or other burnishing tool.

{8} Print and color baby face

Using a computer and printer, print the baby face from the font Oh Baby at 102 point on white cardstock. Color the face and pacifier with colored chalk, lightly applying the chalk with a cotton swab.

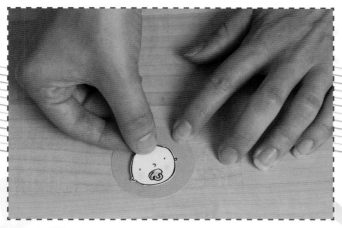

{9} Adhere baby face to tag

Cut the baby face out and adhere it to the center of the light blue circle tag with an adhesive foam dot.

{10} Cut paper strip

Cut a ⁹⁄₁₆" x 3" (14mm x 8cm) strip of pastel striped paper, cutting along the length of the lines.

{11} Add strip to tag

Feed the paper strip through the opening in the blue circle tag so that the stripes face out. Continue feeding until the two ends of the strip are equal on each side, then attach the two ends together with a small safety pin.

{12} Finish card

Insert the circle tag into the slit of the card, sliding the tag in until just the top is visible. At this point, you can use the safety-pinned paper strip as a tab to pull the "Peekaboo" baby face in and out of the card.

New Neighbor Gift Bag

When a new family moves to the neighborhood, make them feel welcome with this special gift bag. Fill the bag with lots of goodies—home-baked cookies, a neighborhood phone directory, school information, a list of local amenities, and maybe even a movie for a night of relaxation after a long day of moving.

MATERIALS AND TOOLS

* white kraft gift bag
* heart template (page 114)
* house template (page 114)
* roof template (page 114)
* decorative text-weight paper (all from *Great Room* collection of Scrapbook Walls, by Chatterbox)

    red large-floral patterned paper (*Scarlet Bloom*)

    multicolored small-floral patterned paper (*Great Room*)

    red-on-red floral patterned paper (*Scarlet Bandana*)

* solid-colored text-weight paper

    solid red paper

    solid golden yellow paper

    solid brown paper

* alphabet stickers (*Just My Type*, by Doodlebug Designs)
* thread: green, golden yellow, rust
* "Home Sweet Home" ribbon
* white fiber
* green acrylic paint (*Evergreen*, Making Memories Scrapbook Colors Paint)
* rust ink pad

* paint sponge
* alphabet stamps (Hero Arts)
* pencil
* metal ruler
* scissors
* craft knife
* self-healing cutting mat
* hole punch
* spray adhesive
* glue stick
* sewing machine
* photocopier

{1} Cut patterned paper

Using a metal ruler and craft knife, cut the following: a 9¾" x 7¾" (25cm x 20cm) piece of red large-floral patterned paper; a 3" x 8½" (8cm x 22cm) piece of multicolored small-floral patterned paper; and a 2½" x 6¾" (6cm x 17cm) piece of solid yellow paper.

{2} Paint paper

Place alphabet stickers along the center of the yellow piece of paper to spell "welcome." Using a paint sponge, paint over the stickers with the green paint, covering the entire surface of the paper. Set aside, allowing to dry for step 6.

{3} Trace and cut out heart and house

Trace the heart template (enlarged at 100%) on solid red paper, the house template (enlarged at 133%) on solid yellow paper, and the roof template (enlarged at 100%) on solid brown paper. Cut out the heart, house and roof. Punch a hole at the top of the heart.

{4} Stamp words on house

Using rust ink and alphabet stamps, stamp the words "to the neighborhood" in the center of the yellow house cutout.

{5} Stitch base page together

Using green thread and a sewing machine set to a straight stitch, sew a border around the red large-floral patterned paper. Use a glue stick to adhere the multicolored small-floral patterned paper to the stitched paper, placing it about ⅝" (16mm) from the top edge and ⅝" (16mm) from the left edge. Stitch a golden yellow zigzag border around the edges, as shown. This is your base page.

{6} Peel off stickers

When the green paint has dried, carefully peel the letter stickers off the painted paper to expose the word "welcome" in yellow.

{7} Add "welcome" to base page

Using rust thread and a sewing machine set to a straight stitch, sew the "welcome" paper to the base page, about 1¾" (4cm) from the top edge and ¼" (6mm) from the left edge.

{8} Embellish house cutout

Wrap a length of white fiber around the yellow house cutout. Hold the two tails of the fiber together, just below the word "neighborhood." Run the fiber tails through the hole of the heart, then tie them in a knot to secure the heart in place.

{9} Sew house to base page

Using green thread and a sewing machine set to a straight stitch, sew the house cutout to the base page, placing it about ¾" (19mm) from the bottom edge and ¾" (19mm) from the right edge.

{10} Sew roof to base page

Using green thread and a sewing machine set to a straight stitch, sew the roof cutout to the base page, placing it right above the house cutout. Trim any excess thread from the page.

{11} Add base page to bag

Coat the back of the base page with spray adhesive, then mount it to the front panel of a white kraft gift bag. Add a decorative "Home Sweet Home" ribbon to the handle, tying it in a bow to secure.

The Art of Gift-Giving

Gifts are always special, but they become even more meaningful when they include a handcrafted touch. Whether you create the container that holds the gift, the card that accompanies it or the gift itself, you can be sure that the extra effort makes all the difference to the recipient. When you incorporate papercrafting techniques into your creations, gift-giving becomes an art.

Avoid last-minute stress by keeping the following tips in mind:

✳ *Keep a calendar, and plan ahead so you have plenty of time to finish the project before the event is celebrated.*

✳ *Consider making several gift-giving containers, such as the New Neighbor Bag, at one time. That way, you will be ready at a moment's notice for the next celebration, even if it pops up unexpectedly.*

✳ *Keep an eye out for unique containers that can be dressed up with your own paper crafting embellishments. It is always fun to receive a gift in something other than a wrapped box.*

Thank-You Card

When somebody takes the time to do something nice for you, isn't it gratifying to put the same kind of thought into your thank-you note? It needn't be anything complicated. This simple but sophisticated handcrafted card is a great way to show your appreciation.

MATERIALS AND TOOLS

* decorative text-weight paper

    pink diamond patterned paper (Paper Wardrobe Boutique Pink Diamond, page 121)

    brown and pink polka-dot patterned paper (Paper Wardrobe Boutique Pink Polka-Dot, page 122)

* solid light pink cardstock

* paper embellishment cutouts (page 117)

    pink border belt

    blue border belt

    "thank you" word box

    decorative paper flower

* pink eyelet
* pencil
* metal ruler
* stylus
* bone folder or other burnishing tool
* scissors
* craft knife
* self-healing cutting mat
* eyelet-setting tools
* glue stick

{1} Cut and fold paper

Cut a 4" x 11" (10cm x 28cm) piece of double-sided (pink/brown) patterned paper. Measure 6" (15cm) over from one of the short sides, then use a stylus and bone folder to score and fold the card.

{2} Add pink strip

Using scissors or a craft knife, trim a pink border belt to 4" (10cm) in length. With a glue stick, glue it on the front flap of the card, placing it flush with the bottom edge.

{3} Add blue strip

Trim a blue border belt to 4" (10cm) in length. Center and glue it on the pink border belt.

{4} Mount paper inside card

Using a metal ruler and a craft knife, cut a 3¼" x 4½" (8cm x 11cm) piece of solid light pink paper. Glue it to the interior panel of the card, placing it about ¼" (6mm) below the inside fold.

{5} Finish interior

Set a pink eyelet in the center of the flower cutout. (For more instruction on setting eyelets, see page 13.) Glue this embellishment to the top center of the paper mounted to the card interior. Adhere a "thank you" word box to the bottom of the card, placing it in the lower right corner.

Remembering

It has been said that the most important word in the English language is "remember." I can see why! We are often so busy that we don't take the time to relish the small moments in our lives—moments that, in retrospect, will mean so much to us. These moments may happen during special celebrations and get-togethers, or during the seemingly humdrum routine of everyday life. Don't let them slip away! The projects in this section provide ways to capture and preserve the memories we make, no matter what the occasion.

Family Reunion Memoir Album

Special gatherings such as family reunions are always perfect photo opportunities. Create this personalized memoir album to hold treasured reunion memories. If you are organizing any large family event, consider making personalized albums for each family to have as a remembrance of the celebration.

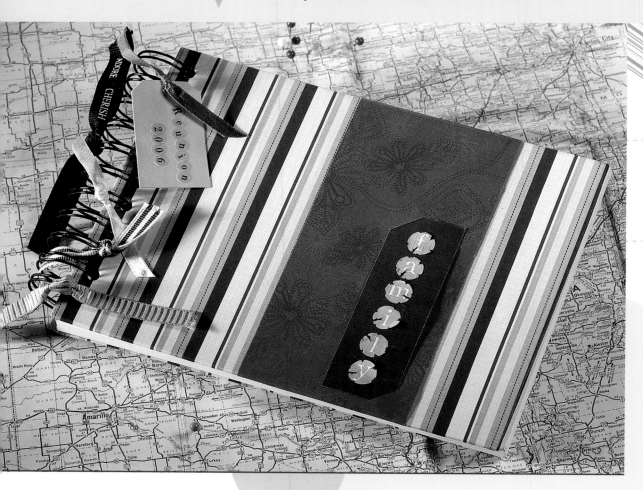

MATERIALS AND TOOLS

* spiral-bound album
* decorative text-weight paper (all from Great Room collection of Scrapbook Walls, by Chatterbox)

    red-on-red floral patterned paper (Scarlet Bandana)

    striped paper (Vest Stripe)

* solid brown text-weight paper
* alphabet stickers (Making Memories)
* "Memories" definition sticker (Making Memories)
* address stickers (Olive "Chippy" Scrapbook Address Stickers, by Chatterbox)

* decorative tags
* decorative ribbon
* pencil
* metal ruler
* scissors
* craft knife
* self-healing cutting mat
* ¼" (6mm) hole punch and hammer
* spray adhesive
* glue stick

{1} Remove covers

Remove the front and back cover from the album, unthreading the spiral binding and keeping both covers intact.

{2} Cover front and back covers

Cut two 8½" x 6½" (22cm x 17cm) pieces of striped paper, making the stripes parallel to the short sides. Lay each paper, striped side down, on your work surface, then coat the back surfaces with spray adhesive. Center each cover, face down, on the paper. Cut a square notch in each corner of the paper, then neatly wrap the flaps over each edge. Flip each cover over and burnish the paper with your fingers to eliminate any air bubbles.

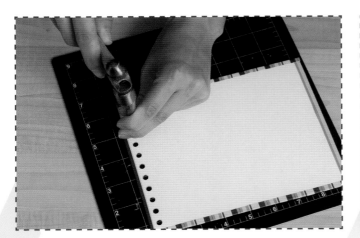

{3} Punch holes through back of cover

Place one cover, paper-side down, on a cutting mat. Insert a ¼" (6mm) hole punch in the holes along the edge of the cover and tap with a hammer, punching through the paper. Repeat with the other cover.

{4} Punch holes through front of cover

Cut two 7¾" x 5¾" (20cm x 15cm) pieces of brown paper. Use spray adhesive to mount the paper to the back of each cover. Place one cover, paper side down, on a cutting mat. Use a ¼" (6mm) hole punch and hammer to punch holes through the cardstock, as you did in the previous step. Repeat with the other cover.

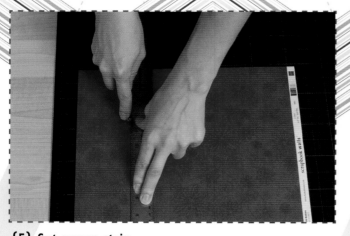

{5} Cut paper strip

Cut a 3" x 12" (8cm x 30cm) strip of red-on-red floral patterned paper.

{6} Prepare title tag

Cut a 1¼" x 3¾" (3cm x 10cm) strip of brown paper. Mount alphabet stickers vertically down the center of the strip to spell "family."

{7} Wrap paper strip around cover

Wrap the red-on-red floral paper strip around one of the covers, folding the strip around the top and bottom edges of the cover. Do not glue.

{8} Trace tag on paper wrap

Unwrap the red-on-red floral strip from the cover and place it vertically on your work surface. Place the brown "family" tag in the lower right corner of the middle panel, about ¼" (6mm) above the bottom fold. Lightly trace around the tag with a pencil, as shown, then remove the tag.

{9} Cut slits in paper wrap

Using a craft knife, cut four ⅝" (16mm) diagonal slits—one in each corner of the tag shape that was just traced onto the red-on-red floral paper strip.

{10} Adhere wrap around cover

Replace the paper wrap around the front cover, as it was in step 7, this time adhering it in place with spray adhesive. (Avoid applying glue over the slits.) On the back of the cover, affix a "memories" definition sticker over the seam where the two edges meet (or almost meet).

{11} Reattach front cover

Reattach the front cover to the album, rethreading it onto the spiral binding.

{12} Reattach back cover

Reattach the back cover to the album, rethreading it onto the spiral binding.

{13} Embellish cover

Attach a decorative ribbon and tag to the spiral binding. Place the "family" title tag on the cover, inserting it into the slits of the paper wrap to secure.

Princess Keepsake Frame

This pretty frame offers the crowning touch for a photograph of your little princess. The design is simple to alter—just change the number to the age of your little one, and, if it's a "prince" instead of a "princess," adjust the color scheme as you see fit!

MATERIALS AND TOOLS

* ready-to-finish memory frame
* pink striped text-weight paper (Pretty Little Girl Stripe Pink, by Wild Asparagus)
* cardstock
    * solid eggplant cardstock
    * solid off-white cardstock
    * solid pink cardstock
* acrylic paint
    * white
    * pink
* glitter paint (Disco Papier Glitter paint, by Plaid)

* princess crown sticker (Sleeping Beauty, by Stickers by Jolee)
* foam number stamp (Gabby Alphabet Foam Stamps, by Making Memories)
* seed bead mix (Sundae Seed Bead, by Lä Dé Dä Designs)
* fine pink glitter
* rhinestones (pink, eggplant and clear)
* pink satin ribbon, ¾"-wide (19mm)
* pencil
* metal ruler
* scissors
* craft knife

* self-healing cutting mat
* spray adhesive
* ultra sticky craft tape sheets (double-sided)
* hot glue gun
* paintbrush
* computer and printer

{1} Prepare frame and trace onto paper

Remove the glass from a memory frame, then basecoat the surface of the frame with white acrylic paint. Allow the paint to dry. Cut a 9" x 6" (23cm x 15cm) piece of striped paper, with the stripes running parallel to the short ends. Lay this paper striped-side down on your work surface, then lay the memory frame face down on the paper. Trace the frame's window onto the paper.

{2} Cut window

Cut the window out of the striped paper, following along the traced lines.

{3} Cut and fold cardstock

Cut a 4" x 9" (10cm x 23cm) strip of eggplant cardstock. Lay the cardstock strip on your work surface horizontally, then place the frame face down on top of it. Line up the long edge (bottom edge) of the frame with the top edge of the cardstock, as shown. Trace the edges of the frame window onto the cardstock, then cut out, following along the traced lines.

{4} Cover frame with paper

Coat the back of the striped paper with spray adhesive, then adhere it to the front of the frame. Coat the back of the eggplant paper with spray adhesive, then adhere it to the front of the frame, along the bottom edge. Adjust the paper as necessary, making sure all the edges line up, then use your fingers to burnish the paper in place.

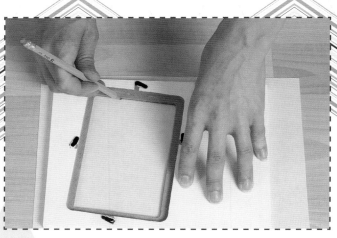

{5} Add ribbon to paper-covered frame

Glue a length of pink satin ribbon over the seam where the two papers meet. Trim the ribbon along the edges of the frame window.

{6} Trace frame onto craft tape

Place a sheet of ultra sticky craft tape, glossy side up, on your work surface, then lay the memory frame face down on top of it. Trace the frame window onto the sheet of tape.

{7} Create craft-tape frame

Use a craft knife to cut out the window, following along the traced lines. Draw a line ¼" (6mm) in from each side, creating a rectangle within the window cutout. Using a craft knife, carefully cut out the center, following along the lines. Remove the interior rectangle; you should now have a ¼"-wide (6mm) craft-tape frame.

{8} Bead craft-tape frame

Peel one backing side off the craft-tape frame, exposing the sticky adhesive surface. Place the frame, sticky-side up, on a sheet of scrap paper. Pour the seed-bead mixture and glitter over the frame until you have covered the surface.

{9} Attach beaded frame to window

Peel the other backing side off the seed bead frame and adhere it to the frame, placing it right around the window so that it frames the opening.

{10} Stamp number on cardstock

Using foam stamps and pink acrylic paint, stamp the number 3 (or other number of your choice) onto a piece of off-white cardstock. Let the paint dry completely.

{11} Outline number

Outline the number with glitter paint, as shown. Let the paint dry, then cut out the number.

{12} Create decorative title tag

Create a decorative title tag on your computer. For this tag, I laid out the words "Our little princess" in the upper half of a 2" x 3" (5cm x 8cm) text box. Print the tag on a piece of off-white cardstock, then trim it to a 2" x 3" (5cm x 8cm) rectangle. Mount the tag onto a piece of pink cardstock. Trim the cardstock, leaving a $^{1}/_{8}$" (3mm) border of pink. Glue the number 3 to the off-white cardstock, directly below the title.

{13} Finish frame with tag and rhinestones

Glue the princess title tag to the frame, adhering it next to the window, as shown. Add a crown sticker to the tag. Finish the frame by adding rhinestones, using a hot glue gun to adhere them to the pink ribbon.

Romantic Keepsake Box

This keepsake box, covered in a charming paisley design, is a wonderful container for storing wedding, anniversary or other romantic mementos. With its customized handmade touch, it could also impress your sweetheart as a Valentine's Day surprise gift box.

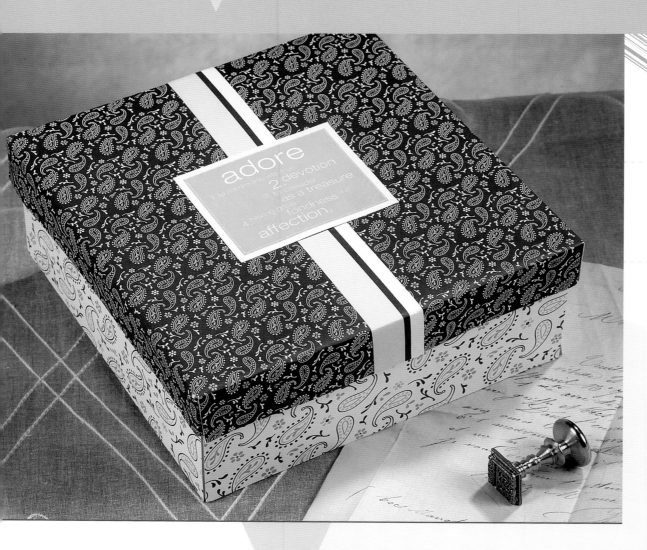

MATERIALS AND TOOLS

* 7½" x 7½" x 3" (19cm x 19cm x 8cm) papier-mâché box, with lid
* decorative text-weight paper (all from *Cosmopolitan* collection, by Making Memories)

    dark paisley patterned paper (*Cosmopolitan Petite Paisley Pink*)

    light paisley patterned paper (*Cosmopolitan Silk Scarf Pink*)

    pink striped paper (*Cosmopolitan Handbag Stripe Pink*)

* solid cream cardstock
* word ("adore") sticker (Making Memories)
* pencil
* metal ruler
* scissors
* craft knife
* self-healing cutting mat
* spray adhesive
* glue stick

{1} Prepare paper

Cut a 9½" x 9½" (24cm x 24cm) piece of dark paisley pat-terned paper. Draw a line 1" (3cm) in from each side of the paper, creating a 7½" x 7½" (19cm x 19cm) square. At each corner, the lines intersect to form a small square. Use scissors to snip along along the left edge of each small square, stopping at the point of intersection, to create flaps.

{2} Cover box lid with paper

Coat the back of the paisley paper with spray adhesive. Lay it on the box lid, centering the square on the lid top. Fold the paper to cover the edges, then wrap the flaps around each corner of the lid and press firmly in place.

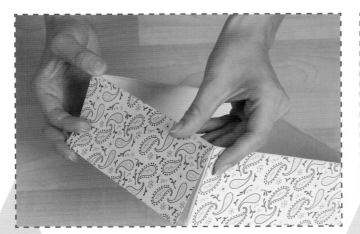

{3} Cover box base with paper

Cut four 2⅞" x 7¼" (7cm x 18cm) pieces of light paisley patterned paper. Coat the back of one piece with spray adhesive, then adhere it to one of the sides of the box base. Repeat with the other three pieces until all four sides of the box base are covered.

{4} Finish box design with paper embellishments

Cut a 1" x 9½" (3cm x 23cm) strip of striped paper and, using a glue stick, adhere it along the center of the box lid. Mount a word sticker (I chose "adore") onto a piece of cream cardstock, then trim the cardstock, leaving a ⅛" (3mm) border around the sticker. Adhere the mounted sticker to the box lid with a glue stick, placing it in the center, over the paper strip.

Accordion-Fold Mini Album

A mini album like this one is such a clever way to store and display small groups of related photos. I customized this album for my children, who love to spend time with their cousins. You can change the title just by choosing a different word tag.

MATERIALS AND TOOLS

* double-sided decorative cardstock (Wild Asparagus)

    solid lime green/ light blue striped cardstock

    solid red/retro floral patterned cardstock

    solid tan/checkered patterned cardstock

* matboard
* word card for book title ("cousins," by Wild Asparagus)
* green ribbon
* red acrylic heart embellishment (Heidi Swapp)
* pencil
* metal ruler
* stylus
* bone folder or other burnishing tool
* scissors
* craft knife
* self-healing cutting mat
* corner-rounder punch
* glue stick
* hot glue gun

{1} Cover boards

Using a craft knife and metal ruler, cut two 7" x 7" (18cm x 18cm) pieces of matboard. For a clean edge, run the knife through the cut two or three times. Cover one side of each board with a 9" x 9" (23cm x 23cm) piece of light blue striped paper.

Note: *Before covering the boards, first cut each corner of the striped paper at a 45° angle, as shown, then neatly fold the flaps over the edges of the board.*

{2} Create back cover

Place one board (which will be the back cover), uncovered side up, on your work surface; set the other one (which will be the front cover) aside for step 5. Using a hot glue gun, adhere a 24" (61cm) length of green ribbon horizontally across the center of the board, allowing about 8½" (22cm) of ribbon to hang off the left edge and 8½" (22cm) of ribbon to hang off the right edge. Set aside for step 9.

{3} Cut and fold cardstock

Cut five 6" x 12" (15cm x 30cm) pieces of double-sided cardstock: two tan/checkered and three red/floral. Score and fold each of these rectangular pieces in half, creating five folded cardstock squares.

{4} Round corners of cardstock

Round the corners of all five folded cardstock squares. (I used a corner-rounder punch, but you can also use scissors.)

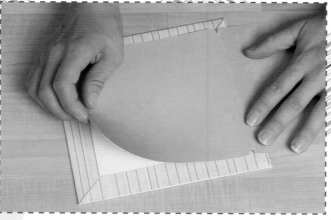

{5} Add cardstock to front cover

Place the other paper-covered board face down on your work surface. Unfold one of the tan/checkered cardstock squares into its original rectangular shape, and lay it on your work surface pattern side up. Coat one half of the cardstock—one of the round-cornered square panels—with a glue stick, then place it centered on the board, as shown. Use your fingers to burnish in place.

{6} Adhere additional layer of cardstock

Fold the unattached side of the tan cardstock over the attached side so that the checkered side is showing. Unfold one of the red/floral cardstock squares into its original rectangular shape and lay it on your work surface pattern side up. Coat one of the tan sides with a glue stick, then adhere it to the checkered cardstock already mounted to the board, aligning the edges perfectly. Burnish.

{7} Add second page onto first page

Turn the piece over and pull the cardstock out to the side of the cover, so that two rust panels are showing. Coat the red panels on the right with glue and attach one of the tan panels. Burnish.

{8} Add third page to second page

Flip the book over. Coat the tan square panel on the end with a glue stick. Adhere the last red/floral rectangle, pattern side up, to the glued-up panel, aligning the edges perfectly.

{9} Attach last page to back cover

Coat the last square panel with a glue stick. Carefully flip the book back over, then adhere the glued-up panel to the uncovered side of the back cover.

{10} Glue and cut out heart

Glue a red acrylic heart embellishment to a scrap of red cardstock. Cut it out, trimming the cardstock along the edges of the heart.

{11} Add title tag

Adhere a text tag or word card of your choice to the front cover, placing it in the lower right corner. (I chose one with the word "cousins.") Glue the heart to the cover, slightly overlapping the tag.

{12} Tie ribbon in bow

Bring the two ends of the back-cover ribbon around to the front of the album and tie a bow, securing the book shut.

CD/DVD Holder

For a special event or celebration, consider creating a personalized compact disc with favorite songs or a custom-made DVD with cherished video clips. The discs can be passed out as party favors, neatly presented in this pretty folding holder.

MATERIALS AND TOOLS

* decorative text-weight paper

  light blue floral paper (Paper Wardrobe Boutique Blue Floral, page 123)

  pinstriped paper (Paper Wardrobe Boutique Pinstripe, page 124)

* light pink cardstock
* paper embellishment cutouts

  pink and brown border

  pink scalloped circle frame

  word cut-out ("remember")

* pink satin ribbon

* brown thread
* stylus
* bone folder or other burnishing tool
* scissors
* craft knife
* self-healing cutting mat
* spray adhesive
* glue stick
* sewing machine
* CD or DVD

{1} Cover and fold base cardstock

Cut a 6" x 11" (15cm x 28cm) piece of blue floral paper. Coat the back of the paper with spray adhesive, then adhere it to a piece of pink cardstock, smoothing out any air bubbles. Trim any excess cardstock along the edges of the floral paper. Score and fold the paper-covered cardstock in half, as shown. This is your base cardstock. When finished, place the base cardstock horizontally on your work surface, pattern side down, to prepare for the next step.

{2} Attach interior corner pocket

With spray adhesive, adhere a piece of pink striped paper to a 5½" x 6" (14cm x 15cm) piece of pink (or scrap) cardstock. Trim any excess paper along the edges of the cardstock. Place the paper-covered cardstock over the bottom right corner of the base cardstock to create a triangular pocket, as shown. Trace and trim the striped paper flush with the edges of the base. Use brown thread and a sewing machine to sew a straight-stitch along the edges, attaching the layers to form a corner pocket. Adhere a brown and pink border belt to the top edge of the pocket, and trim.

{3} Insert disc

Slide the CD or DVD of your choice into the interior pocket, as shown. Fold the base closed.

{4} Close holder with ribbon

Glue a word cutout (I chose the word "remember") to the center of a pink scalloped circle frame cutout. With a craft knife, cut two small horizontal slits in the tag, placing one about ⅛" (3mm) from the top center edge and the other directly opposite, about ⅛" (3mm) from the bottom center edge. Thread a length of pink satin ribbon through the slits and tie it around the card.

POP!
on over to the
Dewberry's for some dynamite
Fourth of July fun!
BBQ, swimming & fireworks
Saturday, July 3
6:00 - 9:00 p.m.

Please bring your swim suits

setting traditions

All families develop their own set of "everyday" traditions, but the traditions that we seem to treasure most are those tied to a holiday celebration. Whether it's a special celebration to ring in the New Year, a neighborhood barbecue for the Fourth of July or a gift exchange on Valentine's Day, everyone has a favorite tradition she eagerly awaits as that time of year rolls around. Let the projects in this section inspire you to continue these traditions—or maybe even start new ones—with renewed vigor!

Valentine's Candy Box

Remember making valentine cards as a kid? A handmade valentine never loses its charm—it comes from the heart, making the sentiment of love extra special. Surprise your sweetie with this cute, easy-to-make box, filled with seasonal goodies.

MATERIALS AND TOOLS

* heart template (page 115)
* white heavy-stock paper candy box
* brown swirl-patterned text-weight paper (Dark Chocolate Swirl, by Chatterbox)
* red micro beads
* fine red glitter
* pink satin ribbon
* scissors
* craft knife
* self-healing cutting mat
* small hole punch
* spray adhesive
* ultra-sticky craft tape sheets (double-sided)
* small treats or candy (to fill box)
* photocopier

{1} Unfold box

Disassemble a heavy-stock paper candy box, carefully peeling apart any adhered areas. When completely unfolded, lay it flat, right side (exterior surface) up.

{2} Cover box with paper

Place a sheet of brown swirl-patterned paper face down on your work surface. Coat the right side of the disassembled box with spray adhesive, then mount it onto the patterned paper. Burnish the paper. Using a craft knife, trim along the edges and slits of the paper-covered box.

{3} Reconstruct box

Reassemble the box, folding and gluing as necessary to secure its shape. Fill the box with your choice of treats, candy or a small gift, then close the lid.

{4} Create beaded heart

Trace the heart template onto a sheet of ultra-sticky craft tape and cut it out. Peel off the adhesive backing, then place the heart, sticky side up, on a piece of scrap paper. Pour beads and glitter over the heart until it is completely covered. (For more instruction on beading, see page 11.)

{5} Finish box with ribbon and heart

Punch a hole in the top center of the heart. Wrap a length of pink satin ribbon around the box. Thread one end of the ribbon through the hole of the heart, then tie the ribbon in a pretty knot or bow, securing the heart in place.

Fourth of July Party Invitation

Put a little bang into your summer festivities! Whether you're hosting a grill-out, a pool party or fireworks display, this "dynamite" invitation will really get your guests excited about the big Independence Day celebration.

POP!
on over to the
Dewberry's for some dynamite
Fourth of July fun!
BBQ, swimming & fireworks
Saturday, July 3
6:00 - 9:00 p.m.
Please bring your swim suits.

MATERIALS AND TOOLS

* star template (page 115)
* paper towel tube
* decorative text-weight paper
    stars-and-stripes patterned vellum (The Paper Wardrobe Summer Sophisticates paper pad, by Plaid)
    red linen paper (The Paper Wardrobe Summer Sophisticates paper pad, by Plaid)
* cardstock
    solid white cardstock
    solid blue cardstock

* red and blue fibers (The Paper Wardrobe Summer Sophisticates Labels and Threads, by Plaid)
* silver pipe cleaner
* pencil
* metal ruler
* scissors
* craft knife
* self-healing cutting mat
* hole punch
* spray adhesive
* hot glue gun

* computer and printer
* photocopier
* optional:
    popping noise makers (to fill tube)
    cotton balls

{1} Cover tube

Cut a paper towel tube in half. Coat one side of a 5½" x 5½" (14cm x 14cm) sheet of white cardstock with spray adhesive, then wrap it around the tube. Cut a 5½" x 5½" (14cm x 14cm) piece of stars-and-stripes patterned vellum. Coat the back of the vellum with spray adhesive, then wrap it around the paper-covered tube.

{2} Cut and punch paper circle

Cut a circle, 5" (13cm) in diameter, out of blue cardstock. With a craft knife, cut a straight line along the diameter line of the circle, stopping at the center point. Punch a hole at the center point.

{3} Form cone

Form a cone shape with the cardstock circle by overlapping the two cut ends. Glue the overlapping ends to secure them. Add a bead of hot glue along one end of the paper-covered tube, then place the cone on the hot glue, pressing down gently to secure the cone in place.

{4} Create star-shaped invitation

Using a computer and printer, design and print your party invitation text. Trace the enlarged star template around the invitation text. Cut it out. With a glue stick, mount the star-shaped invitation onto a sheet of red linen paper. Trim the red linen paper, leaving a border of red around the star.

{5} Assemble invitation

Run a silver pipe cleaner through the hole in the top of the cone. Tie the star-shaped invitation around the pipe cleaner with a piece of red or blue fiber. If desired, fill the inside of the tube with popping noise makers, then stuff cotton balls in the tube to seal the end and keep the noise makers secure. Repeat steps 1–5 to make as many invitations as necessary.

Witch Hat Favor Cone

Hosting a Halloween party? Handing out surprises to trick-or-treaters? Why not do something a little different this year? Filled with Halloween treats, this clever witch hat is sure to be a spellbinding delight for little ghosts and goblins!

MATERIALS AND TOOLS

* witch hat template (page 115)
* hat rim template (page 115)
* decorative text-weight paper

  black starry-sky patterned paper (Spooky Frosty Night Sky, by KI Memories Paper)

  lime green stitch-patterned paper (Spooky Stitched Plaid, by KI Memories Paper)
* purple tissue paper

* orange eyelets
* orange grosgrain ribbon
* green thread
* round metal-rimmed tag
* Halloween-themed rub-on designs (Autumn Wholy Cow!, by Basic Grey)
* pencil
* scissors
* craft knife

* self-healing cutting mat
* eyelet-setting tools
* hole punch
* spray adhesive
* glue stick
* hot glue gun
* photocopier
* treats, to fill cone

{1} Create cone

Trace the hat template (enlarged at 200%), including the dotted line, onto the back of a piece of starry-sky patterned paper, then cut it out. Roll the paper to form a cone, using the dotted line to determine the placement of the paper edge. Run a glue stick over the area where the paper overlaps and press to adhere in place. You may need to add a bead of hot glue to the top of the cone to keep the paper in place.

{2} Create hat rim

Coat the backs of two sheets of lime green stitch-patterned paper with spray adhesive, then adhere the paper together back to back. Trace the hat rim template (enlarged at 200%) onto the lime green paper, and cut it out with scissors or a craft knife.

{3} Attach hat rim to cone

Place the hat rim at the base of the cone, then glue the darts of the hat rim to the inside of the cone.

{4} Add ribbon to hat

Punch two holes on the hat rim, placing them directly opposite one another. Set an orange eyelet in each hole. (For more instruction on setting eyelets, see page 13.) Thread a length of orange ribbon through the two eyelets. Tie a couple of knots on each end to hold the ribbon in place.

{5} Finish and fill hat

Apply a Halloween-themed rub-on design to a round metal-rimmed tag. Attach the tag to the orange ribbon with green thread. Insert a piece of purple tissue paper in the cone, then fill it with your choice of Halloween treats.

Thanksgiving Day Gratitude Book

Why not start a new Thanksgiving tradition this year? During your holiday celebration, ask your family members to name what they're thankful for. Document their contributions in this miniature "gratitude book." Keep the books, and pull them out every year for some reminiscing.

MATERIALS AND TOOLS

* small envelope template (page 116)
* large envelope template (page 116)
* 12" x 12" (30cm x 30cm) sheets of decorative text-weight paper (The Paper Wardrobe Fall Sophisticates paper pad, by Plaid)

   brown houndstooth paper

   orange paisley paper

   brown floral paper

   green plaid paper

   floral/striped paper

   plain striped paper

   solid orange

   solid gray

   solid cream
* solid green cardstock
* "Happy Thanksgiving" label and die-cut tags (The Paper Wardrobe Fall Sophisticates paper pad, by Plaid)
* orange eyelet
* brown embroidery floss
* pencil
* metal ruler
* stylus

* bone folder or other burnishing tool
* scissors
* craft knife
* self-healing cutting mat
* eyelet-setting tools
* spray adhesive
* glue stick
* large needle
* photocopier

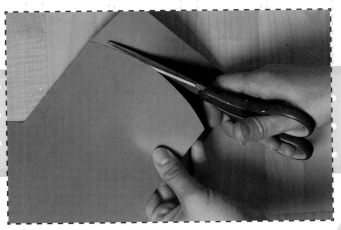

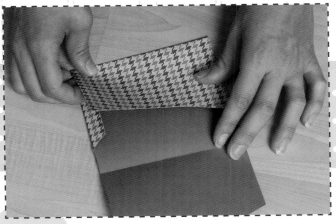

{1} Prepare papers

Adhere the following pairs of 12 x 12" (30cm x 30cm) papers together with spray adhesive: two sheets of brown houndstooth paper, back to back; one brown houndstooth paper onto solid gray paper, back to back; and one brown houndstooth paper onto solid orange paper, back to back. Trace the small envelope template (enlarged at 200%) twice onto the houndstooth/ houndstooth paper, and once onto each of the other papers. (Leave enough room on the houndstooth/orange paper for another template.) Cut out the envelope patterns.

{2} Create small envelopes

Follow along the dotted lines to score and fold each of the four small envelopes, making the gray side the interior. For each envelope, fold in the narrow side flaps first, then apply glue stick to both flaps. Fold up the bottom panel, adhering it to the flaps to form a pocket. Fold down the top panel to complete the envelope.

{3} Create large envelope

Trace the large envelope template (enlarged at 200%) onto the remainder of the houndstooth/orange paper, and cut it out with scissors or a craft knife. Follow along the dotted lines to score and fold the envelope, making the orange side the interior. Fold and adhere the side flaps to the bottom panel as you did in step 2 to form a pocket.

{4} Add orange paper to flap

Leave the large envelope open so that the top panel is not folded down. Cut a 4¼" x 5" (11cm x 13cm) piece of brown houndstooth paper, then glue it to the orange (interior) side of the top panel.

{5} Set eyelet

Place the large envelope, still open, on a cutting mat. Set an orange eyelet in the center of the folded spine. (For more instruction on setting eyelets, see page 13.)

103

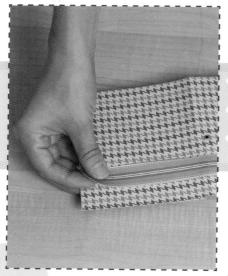

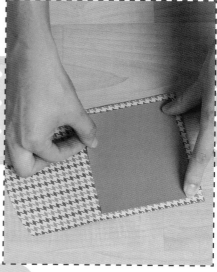

{6} Add paper strip

Flip the large envelope over and place it on your work surface face down. Cut an orange striped strip from a sheet of floral/striped paper. Use a glue stick to adhere it across the exterior of the envelope, placing it about 1" (3cm) above the bottom edge.

{7} Add label

Add a "Happy Thanksgiving" to the front exterior, placing it on top of the orange strip in the lower right corner.

{8} Add cardstock panels to small envelopes

Cut four 5¾" x 4⅜" (15cm x 11cm) pieces of green cardstock. Glue one cardstock piece to the exterior panel of each small envelope.

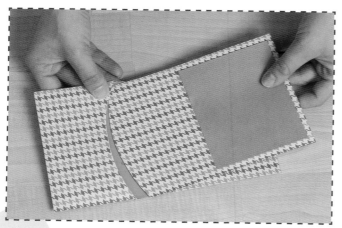

{9} Insert small envelope into large envelope

Open the large envelope and place it on your work surface, pocket side up. Open one of the small envelopes, with the green panel facing up. Slide the top flap of the small envelope into the pocket of the large envelope, as shown.

{10} Insert remaining envelopes

Repeat the previous step with the three remaining small envelopes by sliding each into the pocket of the one before it.

{11} Run floss through center

Thread a piece of brown embroidery floss onto a needle. Run it through the eyelet from the outside of the large envelope to the inside, penetrating through the center of the second envelope.

{12} Run floss around spine

Bring the embroidery floss around the spine, running it over the top of the envelope, around the outside, then back up and through the eyelet from the inside.

{13} Tie floss in knot

Tie the two ends of the floss around the length on the outside spine, forming a knot at the center of the spine on the outside of the large envelope.

{14} Make notecards

Cut a 7" x 4¾" (18cm x 12cm) piece of each of the following papers: orange paisley, brown floral, green plaid, floral/striped and plain striped. Run a glue stick over the back surface of the papers, then fold each in half to create 3½" x 4¾" (9cm x 12cm) double-sided cards. Cut five 2¼" x 4" (6cm x 10cm) pieces of solid cream paper, then glue one cream paper onto each patterned card, placing it about ³⁄₈" (9mm) from one long side.

{15} Slide notecards into envelope

In the ³⁄₈" (9mm) border on each notecard, glue a die-cut tag at the center. Slide each notecard into the pocket of the envelope, with the tags facing up like pull-tabs.

Holiday Candle Holders

These candle decorations will make your holiday season glow. Decorative vellum, which covers the glass cylinders, softens candlelight, adding a quiet but festive atmosphere to any room. Simple but elegant, they are sure to spread the holiday spirit.

MATERIALS AND TOOLS

For first candle holder

* glass cylinder candle holder, 4" (10cm) diameter and 5½ " (14cm) high
* 12" x 12" (30cm x 30cm) sheet of white vellum
* 12" x 12" (30cm x 30cm) sheet of red and green plaid-patterned vellum (The Paper Wardrobe Winter Sophisticates paper pad, by Plaid)
* paisley die-cut tag (The Paper Wardrobe Winter Sophisticates paper pad, by Plaid)
* light green rattail trim
* decorative brad
* pencil

* metal ruler
* scissors
* craft knife
* self-healing cutting mat
* spray adhesive
* pillar candle, to fit inside glass cylinder

For second candle holder

* glass cylinder candle holder
* white vellum
* paisley-patterned/striped text-weight paper (The Paper Wardrobe Winter Sophisticates paper pad, by Plaid)

* poinsettia sticker (Scrapbook Jewelry, by The Paper Wardrobe)
* pencil
* metal ruler
* scissors
* craft knife
* self-healing cutting mat
* spray adhesive
* glue stick
* computer and printer
* pillar candle, to fit inside glass cylinder

{1} Cut vellum for first candle

Using a metal ruler and craft knife, cut a 5 $\frac{13}{16}$" x 12" (15cm x 30cm) strip of white vellum. Coat one side of the vellum with spray adhesive and adhere it to the glass cylinder. (The vellum will not completely cover the glass.)

{2} Cut plaid vellum

Coat the backs of two sheets of plaid-patterned vellum with spray adhesive. Adhere the two sheets together, back to back, making sure that the patterns match exactly. With a craft knife, cut a 5 $\frac{13}{16}$" x 12" (15cm x 30cm) strip across the center diagonal of the double-layered vellum, as shown.

{3} Cover cylinder with plaid vellum

Coat one side of the plaid vellum strip with spray adhesive. Adhere the strip around the cylinder, completely covering the area where the white vellum did not cover the glass.

{4} Embellish cylinder

Wrap a piece of light green rattail trim around the cylinder and tie it in a knot. Push a decorative brad through a paisley die-cut tag, then bend the prongs of the brad around the rattail. Place a pillar candle inside the cylinder.

{5} Create second candle holder

Make a variation of the vellum-covered candle holder, using your choice of embellishments. To do so, first cut a strip of white vellum, making the strip as wide as the height of the glass cylinder and long enough to wrap around the entire surface. Coat one side of the vellum with spray adhesive, then wrap the vellum around the cylinder, adhering it to the glass surface. Use a glue stick to adhere coordinating paper embellishments to the cylinder. Place a pillar candle inside the cylinder.

New Year's Countdown Place Setting

Create a stunning table display for a New Year's Eve dinner party without a lot of expense. Attach name tags to the party crackers and place one on each plate, letting them serve double-duty as fun favors and festive place markers. Then let the countdown to midnight begin!

MATERIALS AND TOOLS

* white posterboard
* decorative text-weight paper

    12" x 12" (30cm x 30cm) silver-on-black pinstriped paper (Designer Silver Pin Stripe, by DieCuts With a View)

    12" x 12" (30cm x 30cm) silver-on-black swirl-and-star patterned paper (Designer Silver Star Swirl, by DieCuts With a View)

    typewriter key patterned paper (Typewriter Alphabet, by Paper Pizazz)

* solid red cardstock
* solid red tissue paper
* paper towel tube
* small silver brad
* round, metal-rimmed tag
* black and red fibers (EK Success Adornments)
* small alphabet stamps (Hero Arts)
* black ink pad
* scissors

* craft knife
* self-healing cutting mat
* spray adhesive
* glue stick
* wine glass
* small treats and party favors, to fill crackers

{1} Adhere paper to posterboard

Cut a 12" x 16" (30cm x 41cm) piece of white posterboard. Use spray adhesive to adhere a 12" x 12" (30cm x 30cm) piece of pinstriped paper in the center, aligning the edges.

{2} Finish covering posterboard to create placemat

Cut two 3½" x 12" (9cm x 30cm) pieces of star-and-swirl patterned paper. Adhere the pieces to the posterboard with spray adhesive, placing one on either side of the pinstriped paper, as shown. This is the placemat.

{3} Embellish placemat

Cut a 1" x 9¾" (3cm x 25cm) strip of red cardstock. Cut letter circles from a sheet of typewriter key patterned paper to spell "celebrate," then adhere the letters to the cardstock strip with a glue stick. Using a small silver brad, attach this strip to the lower left edge of the placemat so that the word "celebrate" runs parallel to the bottom edge.

{4} Make wine glass tag

Cover the center of a metal-rimmed tag with red cardstock, adhering with glue. Use black ink to stamp the word "cheers" in the center of the tag. Once the ink has dried, tie the tag around the stem of a wine glass with black fibers.

{5} Make party cracker

Cut a paper towel tube to 6" (15cm) in length. Place a 12" x 12" (30cm x 30cm) piece of red tissue paper on your work surface, then place the tube, centered, along one edge. Roll the tube with the tissue paper, allowing the paper to cover the tube. Tie one of the paper ends with black and red fibers, then insert treats and favors through the opposite end. When finished, tie the end closed with more fibers. Apply spray adhesive to the back of a 6" x 12" (15cm x 30cm) piece of swirl-patterned paper, and wrap it around the center of the tube to cover.

templates

On the following pages, you'll find handy templates for several of the projects in this book. Use a photocopier to enlarge each template at the appropriate percentage. If, after enlarging the template, you need to trace it onto another sheet of paper, I recommend using a light box. With the illuminated light box as your work surface, the process of tracing is a snap!

Scalloped Circle Template (for Dial-A-Chore Chart, pages 30–31)

Use a photocopier to enlarge pattern 150%.

**Purse Template
(for Purse Party Favor Box,
pages 36–39)**

Use a photocopier to enlarge pattern 160%.

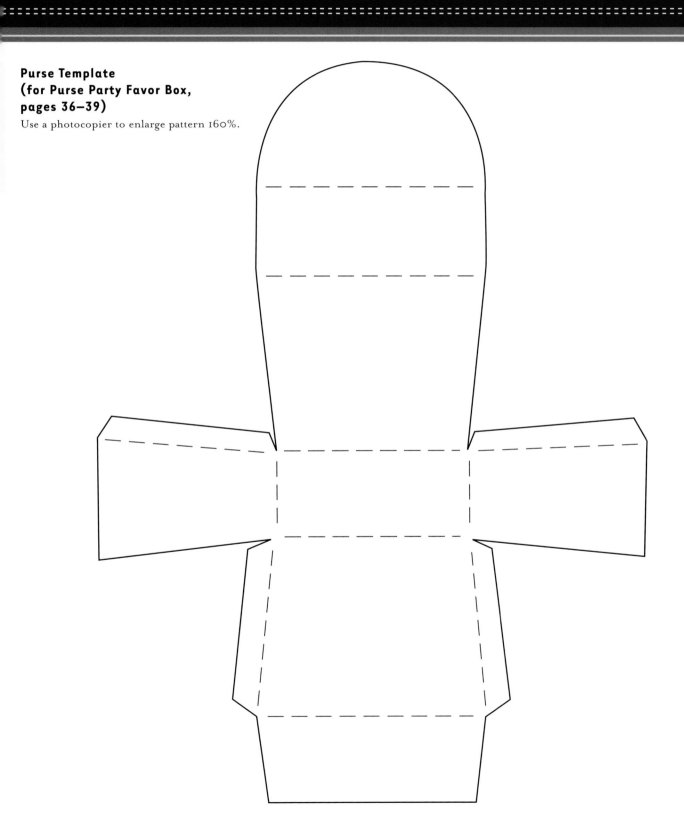

Tag Template
(for Birthday Countdown Frame, pages 42–45, and for Back-to-School Surprise Box, pages 62–65)

Use a photocopier to reproduce pattern at 100%.

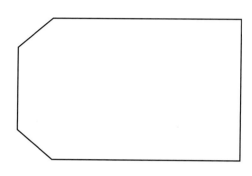

Small Pocket Template
(for Birthday Countdown Frame, pages 42–45)

Use a photocopier to reproduce pattern at 100%.

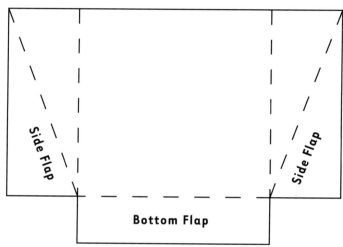

Side Flap

Side Flap

Bottom Flap

Large Pocket Template
(for Birthday Countdown Frame, pages 42–45)

Use a photocopier to enlarge pattern 133%.

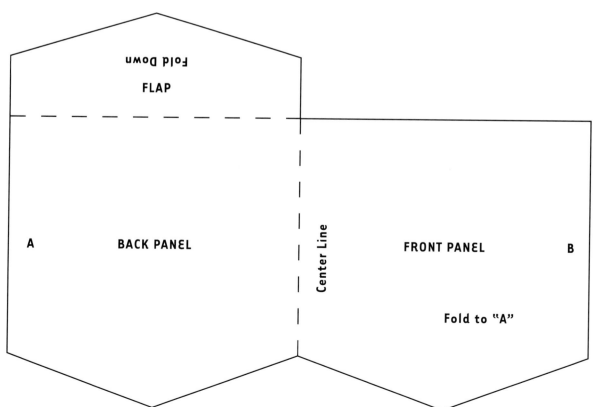

Fold Down

FLAP

A   BACK PANEL

Center Line

FRONT PANEL   B

Fold to "A"

Flip-Flop Template
(for Flip Flop Summer Party Invitation, pages 46–47)

Use a photocopier to enlarge pattern 133%.

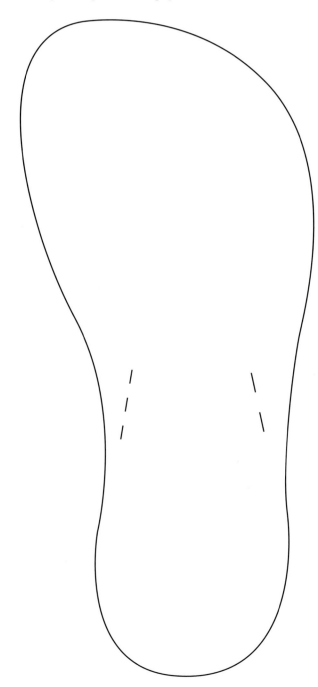

Soccer Ball Template
(for Soccer Party Invitation, pages 48–49)

Use a photocopier to enlarge pattern 133%.

Butterfly Template
(for Butterfly Birthday Card, pages 50–51)

Use a photocopier to enlarge pattern 100%.

Scallop Template (for Lil' Baby Peek-A-Boo Card, pages 66–69)

Use a photocopier to enlarge pattern 133%.

House Template (for New Neighbor Gift Bag, pages 70–73)

Use a photocopier to enlarge pattern 133%.

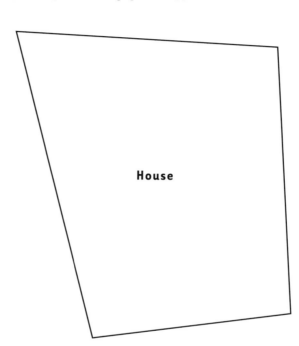

House

Roof Template
(for New Neighbor Gift Bag, pages 70–73)

Use a photocopier to enlarge pattern 100%.

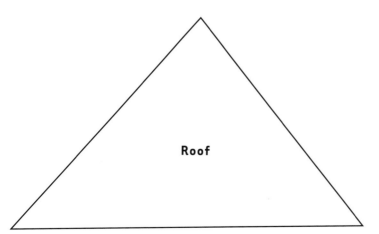

Roof

Heart Template
(for New Neighbor Gift Bag, pages 70–73)

Use a photocopier to enlarge pattern 100%.

Heart

Heart Template
(for Valentine's Candy Box, pages 96–97)

Use a photocopier to reproduce pattern at 100%.

Star Template
(for Fourth of July Party Invitation, pages 98–99)

Use a photocopier to enlarge pattern 150%.

Hat Rim Template
(for Witch Hat Favor Cone, pages 100–101)

Use a photocopier to enlarge pattern 200%.

Witch Hat Template
(for Witch Hat Favor Cone, pages 100–101)

Use a photocopier to enlarge pattern 200%.

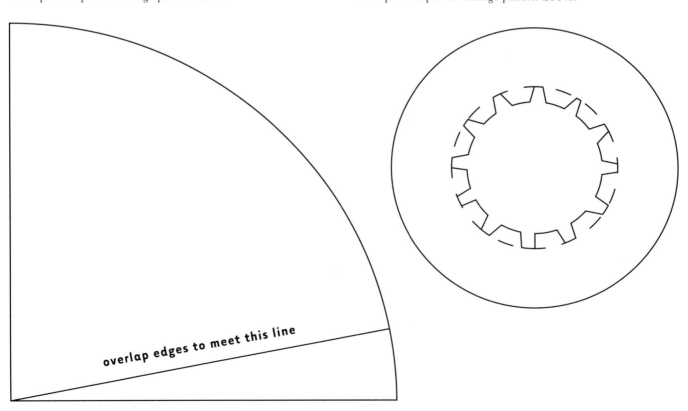

overlap edges to meet this line

Small Envelope Template (for Thanksgiving Day Gratitude Book, pages 102–105)

Use a photocopier to enlarge pattern 200%.

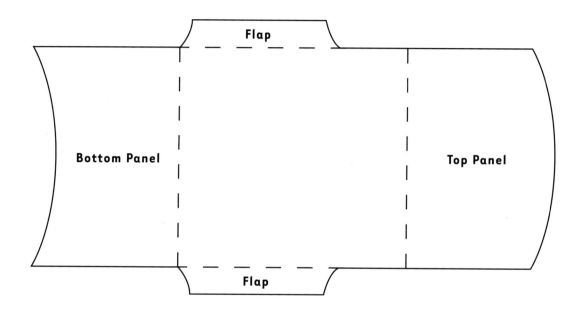

Flap

Bottom Panel

Top Panel

Flap

Large Envelope Template (for Thanksgiving Day Gratitude Book, pages 102–105)

Use a photocopier to enlarge pattern 200%.

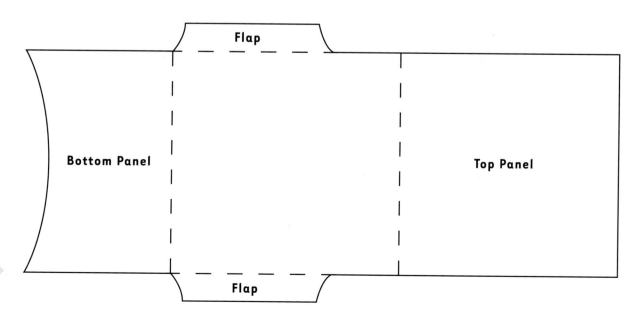

Flap

Bottom Panel

Top Panel

Flap

paper embellishments

CELEBRATE

Thank You

Celebrate

cherish

HAPPY BIRTHDAY

THANKYOU

memories

remember

Thinking of you

paper tear-out section

On the following pages, you will find decorative paper for use in making the Butterfly Birthday Card (pages 50–51), Thank-You Card (pages 74–75) and CD/DVD Holder (pages 92–93). Tear out these sheets, and you'll have ample paper to complete these projects according to the step-by-step instructions. Then, you can use any leftover scraps for your own paper creations or scrapbook pages.

PAPER WARDROBE BOUTIQUE PINK FLORAL

PAPER WARDROBE BOUTIQUE PINK DIAMOND

PAPER WARDROBE BOUTIQUE PINK POLKA-DOT

PAPER WARDROBE BOUTIQUE BLUE FLORAL

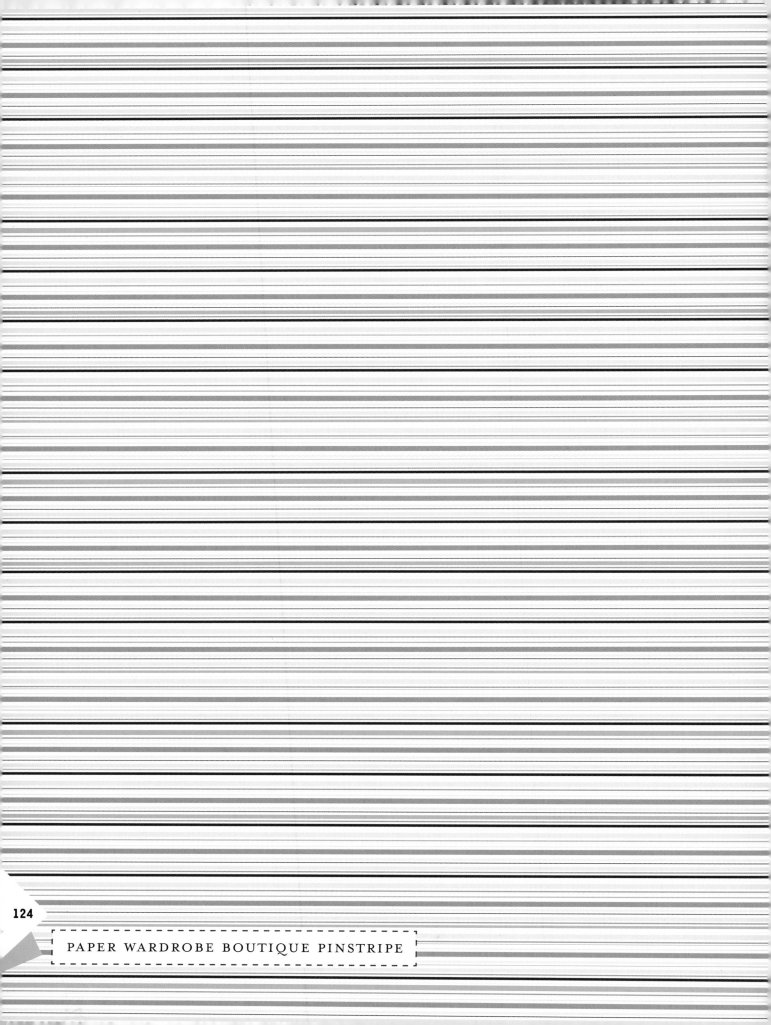

PAPER WARDROBE BOUTIQUE PINSTRIPE

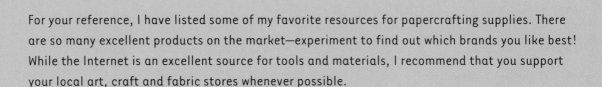

resources

For your reference, I have listed some of my favorite resources for papercrafting supplies. There are so many excellent products on the market—experiment to find out which brands you like best! While the Internet is an excellent source for tools and materials, I recommend that you support your local art, craft and fabric stores whenever possible.

American Crafts
476 North 1500 West, Orem, UT 84057
(801) 226-0747
www.americancrafts.com
pink bubble vellum, argyle ribbon, MetalGrams

Autumn Leaves
14140 Ventura Boulevard #202, Sherman Oaks, CA 91423
(800) 588-6707
www.autumnleaves.com
Wholly Cow Rub-Ons, MOD Designs, Daydream paper collection

Avery
50 Point Drive, Brea, CA 92821
(800) 462-8379
www.avery.com
ink-jet sticker paper, ink-jet magnet paper

Chatterbox, Inc.
1472 Iron Eagle Drive, Eagle, ID 83616
(888) 416-6260
www.chatterboxinc.com
Dark Chocolate Swirl paper, Rosey Pedestal Stripe paper, Great Room paper collection, Chippy scrapbook address stickers

Colorbök
2716 Baker Road, Dexter, MI 48130
(800) 366-4660
www.colorbok.com
My Type printed alphabet conchos

Déjà Views
6 Britton Drive, Bloomfield, CT 06002
(800) 243-8419
www.dejaviews.com
Sharon Ann paper collection

Design Originals
(800) 877-7820
www.d-originals.com
personality word stickers

Die Cuts With a View
2250 North University Parkway #486, Provo, UT 84604
(801) 224-6766
www.diecutswithaview.com
decorative paper

Doodlebug Designs
(877) 800-9190
www.doodlebug.ws
rub-ons, alphabet stickers

EK Success
www.eksuccess.com
Sugar and Spice paper collection and embellishments, fibers

Heidi Swapp
12276 San Jose Boulevard, Building 115, Jacksonville, FL 32223
(904) 482-0092
www.heidiswapp.com
decorative tape, acrylic heart

Hero Arts
1343 Powell Street, Emeryville, CA 94608
www.heroarts.com
alphabet stamps

Karen Foster Design
623 North 1250 West, Centerville, UT 84014
(801) 451-9779
www.karenfosterdesign.com
writing paper

KI Memories
(972) 243-5595
www.kimemories.com
Playful paper collection, Spooky paper collection

Lä Dé Dä Designs
7987 Pecue Lane, Suite I, Baton Rouge, LA 70809
(225) 755-8899
www.ladedadesigns.com
seed beads and glitter

Making Memories
1168 West 500 North, Centerville, UT 84014
(801) 294-0430
www.makingmemories.com
watercolor brads, mini safety pins, scrapbook colors paint, defined stickers, brad alphabet stickers, foam stamps, decorative papers, Signage Petite

Paper Pizazz by Hot Off the Press
2800 Hoover Road, Stevens Point, WI 54492
(888) 300-3406
www.paperwishes.com
Typewriter alphabet paper

Plaid Enterprises, Inc.
3225 Westech Drive, Norcross, GA 30092
(800) 842-4197
www.plaidonline.com
The Paper Wardrobe paper collections and embellishments

Ranger Industries
15 Park Road, Tinton Falls, NJ 07724
(732) 389-3535
www.rangerink.com
Tim Holtz Distress Ink

Scenic Route Paper Company
887 West Center Street, Orem, UT 84057
(801) 225-5754
www.scenicroutepaper.com
Harvest Daisies Chestnut paper

SEI
1717 South 450, Logan, UT 84321
(800) 333-3279
www.shopsei.com
Groovy Gal papers, Table Ticking paper, Granny's Kitchen tabs, polka-dot ribbon

Two Peas in a Bucket
2222 Pleasant View Road, Unit 6, Middleton, WI 53562
(888) 896-7327
www.twopeasinabucket.com
downloadable fonts

Urban Lily
www.urbanlily.com
Frog Spots paper, Mountain Stripe paper, Freestyle Stitch paper

Wild Asparagus
(866) 989-0320
www.mymindseye.com
Cousins paper collection, Pretty Little Girl Stripe pink paper

index

A–B

Adhesives, 9
  glue stick, 9
  hot glue gun, 9
  spray, 9
Albums
  Accordion-Fold Mini, 88
  Baby Journal Calendar, 54
  Family Reunion Memoir, 78
Basic materials and tools, 8
Book, Thanksgiving Day Gratitude, 102
Boxes and containers
  Art Supply Canisters, 24
  Back-to-School Surprise, 62
  Nesting Storage, 20
  Purse Party Favor, 36
  Romantic Keepsake, 86
  Valentine's Candy, 96
Bridal shower invitation, 40

C–D

Calendar, Baby Journal, 54 *See also*
Albums
Candle holders, 106
Cards *See also* Invitations
  birthday, 34, 50
  invitation, 34, 40, 46, 48, 98
  new baby, 66
  thank you, 74
Cardstock or coverstock, 8
Celebrating, 32
  Birthday Countdown Frame, 42
  Birthday Number Invitation, 34
  Butterfly Birthday Card, 50
  Flip-Flop Summer Party Invitation, 46
  Purse Party Favor Box, 36
  Soccer Party Invitation, 48
  "Tying the Knot" Bridal Shower Invitation, 40

Chart, Dial-A-Chore, 30
Cone, Witch Hat Favor, 100

E–H

Event planning, the art of, 39
Favors
  Purse Party, 36
  Witch Hat Cone, 100
File folder, 26
Frames
  Birthday Countdown, 42
  Princess Keepsake, 82
Gift bags
  New Neighbor, 70
  Pretty-in-Pink, 58
Gift-giving, the art of, 73
Giving, 52
  Baby Journal Calendar, 54
  Back-to-School Surprise Box, 62
  Lil' Baby Peek-A-Boo Card, 66
  New Neighbor Gift Bag, 70
  Pretty-in-Pink Gift Bag, 58
  Thank You Card, 74

I–O

Introduction, 6
Invitations
  Birthday Number, 34
  bridal shower, 40
  Fourth of July, 98
  soccer party, 48
  summer party, 46
New Year's Countdown Place Setting, 108
Organizing, 14
  Art Supply Canisters, 24
  Dial-A-Chore Chart, 30
  Greeting Card Organizer, 26
  "Mom's Diner" Dinner Planner, 16
  Nesting Storage Containers, 20
  Personalized Memo Clipboard, 22

P–R

Paper, 8
  heavy-weight, 8
  magnet, 17
  punches for, 9
  specialty printer, 8
  text, 8
  translucent, 8
Paper embellishments, 117
Paper punches, 9
Paper samples, 119
Planner, "Mom's Diner" Dinner, 16 *See also* Organizing
Remembering, 76
  Accordion-Fold Mini Album, 88
  CD/DVD Holder, 92
  Family Reunion Memoir Album, 78
  Princess Keepsake Frame, 82
  Romantic Keepsake Box, 86

S–Z

Setting Traditions, 94
  Fourth of July Party Invitation, 98
  Holiday Candle Holders, 106
  New Year's Countdown Place Setting, 108
  Thanksgiving Day Gratitude Book, 102
  Valentine's Candy Box, 96
  Witch Hat Favor Cone, 100
Techniques, 10
  scoring and folding paper, 10
  setting conchos, 12
  setting eyelets, 13
Templates, 110
Text paper, 8
Translucent paper, 8

Check out these other great books from North Light!

Artful Memories

Carol Wingert and Tena Sprenger

Inside *Artful Memories*, co-authors Carol Wingert and Tena Sprenger show you how to take your memory art to the next level by creatively combining traditional artist's mediums with fabric, papercrafting and book-making supplies. From image transfers to book binding, *Artful Memories* combines the hottest techniques in the memory art world to help crafters make the most of their treasured memories. Choose from over 30 step-by-step projects and get inspired by the fabulous gallery sections for each chapter.

ISBN-10: 1-58180-810-0
ISBN-13: 978-1-58180-810-0
paperback, 128 pages
33488

Sew Easy Papercrafting

Rebekah Meier

In *Sew Easy Papercrafting*, author Rebekah Meier takes you beyond the scrapbook page and shows you how to use fabric, sewing and sewing notions to create 20 beautiful, vintage-style papercrafting projects. Inside, step by step, you'll learn how to create fabulous paper-based projects, from fabric-embellished greeting cards and felt- and lace-covered journals, to paper "crazy quilt" file folders and fabric tag books. With their embellishments of ribbon, bows, buttons and scrapbook charms, each of the projects has a warm, vintage look you'll love.

ISBN-10: 1-58180-772-4
ISBN-13: 978-1-58180-772-1
paperback, 128 pages
33444

Papercrafting Room by Room

Deborah Spofford

If you want intriguing paper projects that go beyond basic cards and gifts, *Papercrafting Room by Room* is for you. This premier book will show you how to turn ordinary home items into extraordinary, stylish pieces. Inside you'll find projects for crafting accents for every room in the house, including embellishing lampshades, clocks, tabletops and more. You'll love using simple techniques such as découpage to add flourish to gorgeous and functional pieces.

ISBN-10: 1-58180-656-6
ISBN-13: 978-1-58180-656-4
paperback, 128 pages
33243

Simply Cards

Sally Traidman

From birthdays to holidays and for all occasions in between, turn to the bright and breezy style of the cards featured in *Simply Cards*. The candy colors, spring brights and retro hues of these cards give them a young, fresh and playful look that's sure to appeal to anyone who receives one of these simple and graphic missives. You'll get maximum yield for minimum time with the cards in this book—just a few basic papercrafting techniqes combined with a little rubber stamping, and voila—the perfect card.

ISBN-10: 1-58180-674-4
ISBN-13: 978-1-58180-674-8
paperback, 128 pages
33260

These books and other fine North Light titles are available at your local craft retailer or bookstore or from online suppliers.